# UNLOCKING YOUR FIRST MILLION

## MUKESH ALEX VAIDYA

BOOKIFY

Book Cover by Pawan Bolor

*This book is dedicated to all my readers*

# CHAPTER 1

It was March 2008, one of the largest IT companies in the world laid me off from my position as a Software Developer. It was nothing my fault. The world was under a severe recession. I was devastated. I had no motivation to apply for another job. And I had no money in the bank to survive.

Exactly seven months before I had the happiest moment in my life, God blessed us with a daughter. In the midst of the great joy I also had to face the greatest despair. There was not a penny in my pocket. I had to pay rent, loan of the car and daily expenses for food and water. I called all my near and dears for help, without any use. First time in my life I hit rock bottom.

It was at that time I stumbled upon Rhonda Byrne's The Secret Movie. I was impressed, motivation kicked in. I realised there was hope. I loaned 100K from my father in law and decided to attract more money with that capital via trading in the financial markets. I studied every books possible about trading and started my new job that was day trading. I exhausted all the capital in less than 3 months. At the same time I realised early in the game that I am a small fish in the ocean where Sharks and Whales rules.

But the crux of the problem for me was the million dollar question why law of attraction is not working for me like hundreds of thousands if not millions. It worked very well for Rhonda and thousands of others. She had recorded one hundred and twenty hours of video but we saw only one hour and thirty minutes. I realised there is something missing from the puzzle. So I started digging into this subject. Taking clue from her own book I realised that it was a book gifted to her by her daughter Hayley that Rhonda started the journey of "The Secret". The book Hayley gave her was The Science of Getting Rich by Wallace D Wattles. It was  more than a century old book. I immediately started reading it. Further research on the subject confirmed that there is a way to attract circumstances and things in life which we desire. There is a perfect way to design our life.

You  can have life where you don't have to answer a boss. You can backpack and travel to your favourite destination. You can live and work from anywhere in the world. You can always enjoy freedom.

Being in the IT industry for more than seventeen years,  finally a day came when I decided to take the plunge to start a software company. It was the beginning of the pandemic in 2020. I bootstrapped my own startup from the home office I had. I had a great product idea. Develop a platform for Food Traceability using Blockchain technology. During the pandemic while all other industries was slowing down IT industry was leaping forward due to the digital transformation the big corporates were forced to implement. This caused a spike in the salary ranges of engineers and I hit on the next road block. Unable to hire the right talent with my budget. My operations slowed down.

But   I got plenty of time to read and write. I decided to follow the white rabbit. Within the next five months I did lot of soul searching and realised that I had a passion from my childhood which was lost due to the conditioning of the fabricated education system. I rekindled my childhood aspirations that was nothing but a passion for reading and writing. I published three books through Amazon KDP. I had very good feedback from those who read the books. I realised this was my path forward. I was convinced that building fortune using writing and publishing the books is possible because my first book a collection of short stories "The Secret of Hiram" became an Amazon Bestseller.

Even though I stumbled on the passion I am born to do.   But what changed my life wasn't a sudden stroke of luck or a groundbreaking idea. It was a shift in how I thought, how I felt, and how I perceived myself and the world around me. It was the moment I stopped seeing myself as a victim of circumstance and started realising I had the power to shape my financial destiny. This shift led to my first million, but more than the money, it led to freedom—a kind of freedom that you, too, can create.

## Understanding Financial Freedom

"Financial freedom" may seem like a buzzword in a world that tosses around phrases like "follow your passion" or "live your best life." But what does it truly mean? Financial freedom is not about never working again or buying a yacht on a whim. Instead, it's the state of being where you have enough wealth, investments, and income sources that you're no longer shackled by the need to trade your time directly for money. Financial freedom is having options -  options to work if you choose, to spend time with family, to pursue hobbies, to travel, or even to support causes close to your heart.

But for many, financial freedom feels as distant as a dream. Breaking out of the traditional paycheque to paycheque lifestyle can seem insurmountable, but it often begins with a very tangible, achievable milestone: making your first million.

In the words of Sarah, a single mother from Philadelphia who struggled for years, financial freedom began with a dream of simply having enough to keep her and her daughter secure. "When I started out, all I wanted was stability," she recalls. "My million-dollar goal seemed like a fantasy back then, but I knew it would be the turning point for us." For Sarah, that first million didn't just change her finances; it transformed her outlook on life. Today, her wealth allows her to send her daughter to college debt-free and work because she wants to, not because she has to.

## The Importance of Your First Million

Why the million-dollar milestone? It's a number that resonates with many because it's large enough to significantly shift your financial circumstances and small enough to be within reach, even if it takes years of effort. That first million is more than a dollar amount; it represents a psychological shift. It's a point where you start to understand that, yes, wealth is possible, and you can achieve financial freedom if you approach it step-by-step.

Imagine John, who began his journey with just $300 in savings and a desire to change his life. John worked as a bartender in his twenties, making enough to cover rent and go out with friends on weekends. Saving was rarely on his mind. But as he entered his thirties, he realized he wanted something more stable, a career that could allow him freedom in his future. "I got tired of feeling like I was just drifting through life," John says.

John's journey toward his first million was not overnight. He invested in learning a new skill: digital marketing. He dedicated countless hours to mastering SEO, building websites, and eventually landing higher-paying clients. As his knowledge grew, so did his income. By his early forties, John's hard work and investments had paid off. He didn't just reach his first million — he far surpassed it.

For John, reaching that million-dollar milestone was about more than just a number. It gave him options. Today, John spends his time traveling the world, working only when he wants to, and giving back to causes he cares about. His story is one of countless examples where determination, smart choices, and a commitment to a goal have changed the course of a life.

## Defining Financial Freedom for Yourself

Your version of financial freedom may look different from John's or Sarah's. Some people imagine freedom as never working again, while others see it as having the freedom to choose the work they're most passionate about. Financial freedom doesn't have a one-size-fits-all definition, and this is an important realization as you embark on your journey to your first million. Take some time to think about what financial freedom would look like for you. Is it being debt-free? Retiring early? Having the ability to support family members or causes close to your heart?

## From Scarcity to Abundance: Shifting the Money Mindset

Most people grow up with a scarcity mindset about money. We're taught to save every penny, work hard, and avoid financial risks. And while these pieces of advice have their place, a scarcity mindset can also hold you back from achieving true financial freedom.

Take Emma, a teacher in rural Texas. She grew up in a family that lived paycheque to paycheque, where the focus was on cutting expenses rather than expanding income. Emma, however, dared to break this cycle. She began selling online courses, sharing her teaching expertise with a global audience. At first, it was a side project, generating a modest income, but she eventually built it into a six-figure revenue stream. By her mid-thirties, she was well on her way to making her first million. Emma's story is a powerful reminder that changing how you think about money — from scarcity to abundance — can be a life-changing decision.

When you view money from an abundance perspective, you recognize that wealth is achievable and that money isn't something that's limited or "out of reach." Rather than fearing financial risks, you learn to assess and manage them. And as Emma found, this shift in mindset is essential on the path to your first million.

## Setting Your Sights on the Million-Dollar Mark

Building your first million can be a process filled with hard work, persistence, and determination. It may take years, or it could happen within months, depending on your choices and circumstances. Your journey may include setbacks, disappointments, and recalibration, but the key is to keep moving forward.

Here's a story about Chris, a young father from Los Angeles, who made his first million from a startup. Chris had a stable job in marketing but always had an entrepreneurial spirit. With a background in app development, he decided to create a small tool for freelancers to track their projects more efficiently. It was a niche idea, but he believed in its potential. After hours of coding after his day job, Chris launched his app, but it failed to attract users initially. For months, he worked on the feedback, tweaking features, and marketing the app until it finally gained traction.

Within two years, Chris's app reached thousands of users, and he had offers from larger companies interested in acquiring it. By the time he hit that million-dollar mark, Chris wasn't the same person who started out. He had learned to trust his instincts, take calculated risks, and stay resilient in the face of challenges. His journey, like those of Sarah, John, and Emma, exemplifies that making your first million isn't about luck. It's about determination, persistence, and a belief that your efforts will pay off.

## The First Million as a Mindset Shift

Achieving that first million changes your perspective. You realize that wealth is within your reach, that it's possible for you to create a life of abundance, and that financial freedom is not just for the "lucky few." This milestone often marks a major psychological shift. You begin to feel empowered, capable, and aware of your financial choices. It's no longer just about "making it"; it's about transforming your mindset to see that the journey to financial freedom is within your control.

Reaching your first million is an achievement in itself, but more importantly, it sets the foundation for future wealth. You'll discover strategies and habits that work for you, develop resilience against setbacks, and gain confidence in managing your finances. And as John, Sarah, Emma, and Chris have shown, once you make that first million, the next financial milestones become significantly more attainable.

Key Takeaways: Why Your First Million Matters

1. It's a Psychological Milestone - The first million proves that wealth and financial freedom are achievable. It gives you confidence to aim higher and explore new financial possibilities.

2. It Opens Doors to Financial Options - Once you reach your first million, you have a level of stability and choices. You might choose to reinvest, start a business, or take on projects that fulfil you personally and professionally.

3. It Transforms Your Money Mindset - Achieving your first million helps you transition from a scarcity mindset to an abundance mindset. You start seeing opportunities rather than limitations.

4. It Serves as a Springboard - That first million can be the stepping stone toward even greater financial goals. With the habits, discipline, and confidence you gain, future milestones feel much more achievable.

The Psychological Benefits of Achieving Your First Million

When people talk about becoming a millionaire, the focus often falls on material gains. But the truth is, the first million isn't just about having a seven-figure bank balance; it's about the psychological transformation that comes with achieving a major financial milestone. This shift doesn't just alter your finances — it can change the way you approach life, work, and personal growth.

## 1. Self-Confidence and Empowerment

One of the most profound psychological benefits of making your first million is the surge in self-confidence. Hitting a financial goal of this magnitude reaffirms your abilities, decision-making skills, and resilience. You've set a difficult target, likely encountered obstacles along the way, and yet you persevered. Achieving the million-dollar mark shows you that you have the power to create significant change in your life. This newfound confidence can have a ripple effect, empowering you to pursue even bigger goals, make bolder choices, and take calculated risks.

For instance, consider Elena, who grew up in a low-income household and worked multiple jobs to make ends meet. After years of investing in herself, building skills, and making strategic financial moves, she hit her first million at age 36. She says, "I've always had doubts about my worth and ability. But now, I feel like I've proven to myself that I am capable of achieving whatever I set my mind to." Her financial success provided not only security but also a belief in her own resilience and capabilities.

## 2. Freedom from Financial Anxiety

One of the most immediate psychological benefits of reaching your first million is the reduction of financial anxiety. For many, constant worry about bills, debt, and unexpected expenses is a source of daily stress. Having a million-dollar safety net brings peace of mind. You no longer feel the same pressure to take jobs purely out of necessity or endure uncomfortable situations just for a paycheque. Instead, you're in control.

Financial freedom allows you to plan your life with more certainty. Knowing you have a substantial cushion gives you breathing room to make choices based on what truly matters to you, rather than out of financial desperation. Studies have shown that financial security contributes to a healthier mental state, as it alleviates the constant background worry that weighs heavily on many people's minds.

## 3. A Mindset of Abundance

When you achieve your first million, you start to see the world differently. Rather than viewing money as a scarce resource, you start to understand that wealth is something that can be created, grown, and managed. This shift to an abundance mindset allows you to look at challenges as opportunities. You're more likely to take calculated risks because you understand that setbacks are not the end of the road but part of the journey to further wealth and freedom.

People who have achieved financial milestones often report feeling more optimistic and open to possibilities. This abundance mindset also reduces the jealousy or envy that often accompanies financial comparison, allowing you to focus on your own goals and progress rather than feeling insecure or inadequate by others' success.

4. Enhanced Sense of Purpose and Vision

For many, reaching the million-dollar mark provides a sense of purpose and opens up the potential for a bigger vision. Once you've achieved a significant financial milestone, you begin to think beyond personal gain. What else can you accomplish? How can you make a meaningful impact on the lives of others? Many self-made millionaires are driven by a desire to give back or to create something that lasts beyond themselves.

Take James, who reached his first million through investments in renewable energy. Hitting that financial target gave him a new perspective: "Once I realized I had enough for my own needs, I started thinking about how I could use my knowledge and resources to make a difference." For James, the financial milestone helped clarify his purpose, leading him to found a nonprofit focused on sustainable energy solutions. Reaching your first million often reveals a deeper sense of motivation that goes beyond accumulating wealth.

## The Practical Benefits of Achieving Your First Million

While the psychological benefits are profound, the practical advantages of achieving a million dollars are equally impactful. This wealth milestone opens up real, tangible opportunities that simply aren't available at lower income levels.

1. Increased Financial Security and Stability

Practically speaking, having a million dollars in assets provides a significant safety net against life's inevitable uncertainties. Whether it's a health emergency, an unexpected job loss, or a sudden need to care for family members, your financial stability allows you to navigate these events without major disruption to your lifestyle. Unlike those living paycheque to paycheque, you have the means to weather financial storms.

Moreover, reaching a million dollars often leads people to make smarter decisions about insurance, estate planning, and retirement. You're not just living for today; you're actively planning for the future, ensuring that the wealth you've built will continue to provide for you and your loved ones.

## 2. Ability to Invest in Wealth-Building Opportunities

A million-dollar net worth opens doors to investment opportunities that may not be accessible to people with less capital. From real estate and stocks to private equity and even small business ventures, the options for growing your wealth multiply once you reach this milestone. You can afford to take on higher-yield investments, which often come with higher entry costs but offer greater returns.

For example, Carlos, an engineer who made his first million through tech investments, diversified into real estate once he had more capital. This allowed him to leverage his existing wealth and grow it through passive income. His first million provided him with the capital to invest in properties that would generate additional cash flow, giving him the ability to increase his net worth steadily over time.

## 3. Increased Career Flexibility and Choice

Achieving your first million gives you the freedom to make career choices based on fulfillment rather than financial need. You may decide to reduce your work hours, start a passion project, or switch fields entirely without the fear of financial instability. You no longer feel forced to work in situations that don't align with your values, allowing you to prioritise what truly matters to you.

Consider Linda, who spent years climbing the corporate ladder. By the time she reached her million-dollar goal, she decided to step back from the relentless pace of her career to start her own consulting business. This allowed her to work on her terms, giving her a sense of control and purpose that her corporate job lacked. Her first million provided her with the flexibility to make meaningful career decisions.

4. Power to Give Back and Make a Difference

Another practical benefit of reaching the million-dollar mark is the ability to give back. Whether it's supporting charities, helping family members, or investing in community initiatives, financial freedom enables you to contribute in ways that are meaningful to you. Many people find immense satisfaction in using their wealth to make a positive impact on others' lives, and the practical ability to do so often becomes a driving force for continued financial growth.

For instance, Karen, a former teacher who became a millionaire through investing, now funds scholarships for underprivileged students. Her first million not only changed her life but also allowed her to invest in others' futures. Her wealth gave her the means to contribute to a cause she cared deeply about, creating a lasting legacy.

5. Improved Quality of Life

With the financial pressure lifted, you can invest in experiences, health, education, and relationships. Financial freedom means being able to prioritise a lifestyle that brings you joy and fulfillment. From taking trips to dedicating time to hobbies or spending more time with family, a million dollars provides options to enrich your life in ways that don't come with the same financial constraints.

Shifting from a Scarcity Mindset to an Abundance Mindset

A scarcity mindset is rooted in the belief that resources — including money, time, and opportunities — are limited. This belief often manifests as fear and a reluctance to take risks. An abundance mindset, on the other hand, is the belief that there are enough resources for everyone and that wealth, success, and opportunities are not finite. When you adopt an abundance mindset, you see possibilities rather than limitations, which allows you to approach life with optimism, confidence, and a willingness to explore opportunities.

Shifting from scarcity to abundance isn't just about changing your thoughts; it's a profound change in how you approach your goals, relationships, and challenges. Let's explore the journey of this shift and its impact.

## Understanding the Scarcity Mindset

A scarcity mindset is typically shaped by early experiences or societal messages about money and success. For many people, growing up in households where money was tight fosters a deep-rooted belief that wealth is unattainable or requires constant sacrifice. In a scarcity mindset:

Fear of loss dominates. People with a scarcity mindset often focus more on what they could lose than what they could gain. This fear of loss can make them avoid taking risks, even calculated ones that could lead to growth.

Competition feels necessary. Because they believe resources are limited, those with a scarcity mindset may feel the need to compete rather than collaborate, assuming someone else's success diminishes their own.

Money is seen as a zero-sum game. For someone in a scarcity mindset, wealth is a pie with only so many slices to go around. If someone else gets more, it means there's less for them.

For instance, Rebecca, a young professional from a modest background, entered the workforce with the belief that saving every penny was the only way to secure her future. She lived with an intense fear of financial failure, avoiding investments or growth opportunities. While her carefulness helped her save a little, it also prevented her from building significant wealth because she wasn't open to the potential of increasing her income through new skills or investments.

## The Abundance Mindset: Seeing Wealth as Limitless

An abundance mindset is rooted in the belief that resources are limitless and that success is accessible to everyone willing to pursue it. People with an abundance mindset don't just focus on what they have; they focus on what's possible.

An abundance mindset operates with these core beliefs:

Opportunities are everywhere. Those with an abundance mindset understand that there are multiple ways to generate income and build wealth. They believe in learning new skills, investing in assets, and exploring different ventures.

Collaboration over competition. People who adopt an abundance mindset seek to learn from others and share their knowledge. They recognize that others' success doesn't take away from their own and are open to forming alliances and partnerships.

Money as a tool, not a goal. For those with an abundance mindset, wealth is seen as a means to live a fulfilling life, not an end goal. They see money as a tool to achieve freedom, security, and the ability to contribute to causes they care about.

Take Michael, a freelance designer who used to live paycheque to paycheque. After reading about successful entrepreneurs and rethinking his relationship with money, he decided to invest in learning digital marketing and expanding his client base. He began to see his skills as assets and his time as an investment. Over time, he shifted from scarcity, where he feared spending money, to abundance, where he saw spending as a way to build and grow. This shift transformed his finances and increased his income tenfold over five years.

Shifting from a scarcity mindset to an abundance mindset takes conscious effort and often involves reframing deep-seated beliefs. Here are some strategies to make this transition:

## 1. Change Your Language Around Money

The way you talk about money can reinforce either scarcity or abundance. Rather than saying, "I can't afford this," try, "How can I afford this?" This simple shift opens your mind to finding solutions. By rephrasing, you move from a mindset of limitation to one of exploration and opportunity.

## 2. Focus on Value, Not Just Cost

People with a scarcity mindset often fixate on the cost of things rather than their value. For example, someone in a scarcity mindset might see investing in a course as an unnecessary expense. But with an abundance mindset, that same course is seen as an investment in knowledge that could open doors to higher-paying jobs or new income streams. Ask yourself, "What value does this bring?" instead of just "What does this cost?"

## 3. Practice Gratitude Daily

Gratitude is a powerful tool for cultivating abundance. When you focus on what you have rather than what you lack, you naturally start to feel more secure and optimistic. Practicing gratitude helps to quiet the constant need for "more" and refocuses your energy on appreciating what's already available to you. As you do so, you begin to notice new possibilities and potential around you.

4. Surround Yourself with Abundance-Minded People

Surrounding yourself with people who think abundantly can influence your mindset in positive ways. People who believe in growth, opportunities, and success can help shift your perspective and challenge your old beliefs. Consider joining networking groups, masterminds, or communities where people are actively pursuing growth and celebrating each other's successes.

5. Learn to See Setbacks as Growth Opportunities

In a scarcity mindset, failures are seen as dead ends. But with an abundance mindset, setbacks become lessons and stepping stones toward success. People with an abundance mindset see failure as a natural part of progress. They analyze what went wrong, learn from it, and use those insights to make better decisions in the future.

For example, Sarah, an aspiring entrepreneur, failed at her first two business attempts. Her scarcity mindset told her to give up. But as she learned to see her mistakes as lessons, she gained valuable experience that helped her create a successful third business. This perspective shift allowed her to take calculated risks, leading to her first million.

6. Invest in Yourself

People with a scarcity mindset often shy away from investing in their own growth because they see it as an expense rather than an asset. But one of the best ways to cultivate an abundance mindset is by investing in yourself. This could be through formal education, courses, networking events, or even health and wellness. When you view yourself as a valuable asset, you're more likely to see your potential and take steps to increase it.

7. Visualise a Wealthy, Fulfilled Life

Visualising a future where you've achieved financial freedom can help reinforce an abundance mindset. Imagine yourself living a life where money isn't a worry and opportunities are abundant. Picture the career, relationships, and experiences that you'll be able to enjoy. This visualisation practice can help reframe your beliefs about money and motivate you to take steps toward that abundant future.

The Impact of Adopting an Abundance Mindset

1. Improved Financial Decision-Making

With an abundance mindset, you start to make financial decisions based on growth and value rather than fear and limitation. You're more open to investing, exploring new ventures, or spending on experiences that enrich your life. This openness often leads to a healthier relationship with money and a stronger path to building wealth.

2. Greater Resilience and Adaptability

When you believe opportunities are abundant, you become more resilient in the face of setbacks. Rather than giving up after a failure, you're motivated to learn, adapt, and try again. This adaptability is crucial for achieving long-term financial success and stability.

3. Enhanced Relationships and Opportunities

An abundance mindset leads to more supportive and collaborative relationships. Rather than viewing others as competition, you see them as potential collaborators and allies. This can lead to networking opportunities, partnerships, and connections that could eventually contribute to your financial goals.

4. More Fulfilling Pursuit of Wealth

Pursuing wealth from a place of abundance is more fulfilling and less stressful than pursuing it out of fear of lack. When your actions are driven by abundance, you feel more aligned with your values and are motivated by purpose rather than just the need for security. This shift in motivation often leads to a more meaningful and satisfying journey toward financial freedom.

In summary, shifting from a scarcity mindset to an abundance mindset is about reframing your perspective on money, success, and resources. This shift not only transforms your approach to wealth-building but also influences your confidence, resilience, and satisfaction in life. Adopting an abundance mindset creates a strong foundation for reaching — and going beyond — your first million, as it enables you to embrace growth, seize opportunities, and live a life rich in purpose and possibility.

# CHAPTER 2

## Setting Realistic Goals and Building a Wealth Mindset

Making a million dollars might sound like a daunting goal, especially if you're starting from scratch. It's a figure that feels substantial, a milestone that often seems far out of reach. But breaking it down into smaller, actionable steps makes it feel attainable and creates a path you can realistically follow. In this chapter, we'll delve into the importance of setting realistic goals, aligning those goals with a wealth-building mindset, and taking small, strategic actions that can lead to your first million.

To set realistic financial goals, it's essential to understand both the psychology behind wealth-building and the practical ways to create a foundation of sustainable financial habits. Let's begin by exploring what a wealth mindset looks like in action and how it has helped others turn their million-dollar dreams into reality.

### Breaking Down the Million-Dollar Goal into Achievable Steps

Rather than viewing the million-dollar target as one big leap, think of it as a series of smaller, manageable steps. A goal like "I want to make a million dollars" can feel overwhelming if you don't have a clear plan, but breaking it down makes it both actionable and motivating. This approach is often referred to as "goal chunking" – breaking down a large goal into smaller, measurable targets that are easier to track.

Step 1: Start by Calculating the "How"

To hit a million, you need to understand the numbers behind it. Instead of focusing on a million as one lump sum, let's look at how you could reach it in increments. For example:

- $1,000,000 over 10 years requires saving or earning $100,000 each year.

- $1,000,000 over 5 years means bringing in $200,000 annually.

- $1,000,000 over 3 years requires roughly $333,000 each year.

By breaking down the timeframe, you can start to reverse-engineer what actions and earnings will be necessary to meet each milestone.

Step 2: Establish Incremental Financial Goals

Let's look at a story of a young entrepreneur, Sarah, who used goal chunking to meet her million-dollar target. When Sarah started her graphic design business, she set a five-year goal to make her first million. But instead of obsessing over the seven-figure target, she focused on what she needed to earn each year, month, and even week.

For Sarah, the first milestone was earning $100,000 within the first year. She created a plan to sell her services to five new clients each month, charging each one around $1,700. By hitting her monthly targets, Sarah felt like she was making real progress toward her ultimate goal without feeling overwhelmed by the bigger number.

This approach allowed Sarah to keep momentum, even when she hit setbacks. When one client fell through or a project was delayed, she simply recalculated her monthly goal and adjusted her marketing to fill in the gaps. By chunking her goals, Sarah was able to focus on smaller, tangible achievements while keeping her eye on the million-dollar prize.

## Cultivating a Wealth Mindset

Building wealth isn't just about hitting income targets — it's about shifting your mentality and habits to consistently align with your financial goals. A wealth mindset is the belief that you can create and grow wealth over time through deliberate actions. It's a mindset of patience, discipline, and long-term focus. Here's how to begin cultivating this mindset:

### 1. Define What Wealth Means to You

Wealth means different things to different people. For some, it's having enough money to live comfortably without debt. For others, it's financial independence and the ability to make decisions free from financial constraints. Defining what wealth means to you provides clarity and keeps you motivated, especially on challenging days.

For instance, Tom, a software developer, grew up in a family where financial struggle was a constant. He initially set a goal of becoming a millionaire, but what kept him motivated was his vision of what wealth represented: freedom to travel, support his parents, and eventually retire comfortably. By keeping his "why" in mind, Tom was able to focus not just on income but also on building a sustainable wealth strategy that aligned with his long-term goals.

### 2. Practice Patience and Long-Term Thinking

A wealth mindset isn't built overnight. It involves the habit of deferring short-term gratification for long-term gains. People who succeed in accumulating wealth often make intentional decisions to save, invest, and grow their assets rather than spending on immediate comforts.

Consider Elena, a nurse who wanted to make her first million not just to "be rich," but to ensure a secure retirement. Instead of splurging on luxury items after a year-end bonus, she invested the money into a retirement fund. Over the years, this practice compounded her savings, pushing her closer to her million-dollar goal while giving her peace of mind about her future.

Patience and consistent small investments over time can be powerful tools. A wealth mindset recognizes that a little saved or invested today can multiply over years, bringing you closer to your long-term financial goals.

3. Embrace a Growth Mindset

A key component of a wealth mindset is a growth mindset — the belief that you can develop your abilities and increase your knowledge over time. People with a growth mindset view challenges as opportunities to learn rather than as roadblocks. This mindset applies especially well to building wealth.

Take Raj, a high school teacher, who decided to build wealth through real estate. Initially, he had limited knowledge of the housing market, but he committed to learning about investments, property value, and rental income. He attended workshops, listened to podcasts, and shadowed experienced investors. Over time, he learned enough to buy his first rental property, which began generating passive income. Raj's growth mindset allowed him to see that his potential wasn't fixed; he could learn, improve, and grow his wealth by acquiring new skills.

Breaking Goals Down by Building Skills and Increasing Income Streams

One way to turn your million-dollar goal into a concrete plan is to look at ways to expand your skill set and diversify your income streams. This approach involves continuously identifying areas where you can improve or expand, allowing you to increase your earning potential over time.

1. Invest in Skills that Yield High Returns

Certain skills, like sales, digital marketing, data analysis, and public speaking, tend to yield high returns because they're in high demand. By investing time and effort into mastering a valuable skill, you're equipping yourself with a tool that can increase your income.

For example, Lily, an administrative assistant, decided to learn data analysis through online courses. After six months of study, she applied for a higher-paying role within her company, effectively doubling her salary. This extra income allowed her to save more aggressively, bringing her closer to her million-dollar target much faster than if she had stayed in her original position. By focusing on skill-building, Lily significantly accelerated her journey to financial freedom.

2. Diversify Income Streams

Creating multiple streams of income provides a safety net and accelerates wealth-building. This can include side hustles, freelance work, investments, or even passive income sources.

Josh, an accountant, set a goal to make his first million within 15 years. Initially, his income came solely from his accounting job. However, by his third year, he began exploring additional sources of income, such as investing in stocks and starting a small business with a friend. This diversification increased his cash flow and made his wealth-building plan more resilient.

While it might seem challenging to juggle multiple income streams, diversifying income is often a reliable way to accumulate wealth faster. This approach requires diligence and time management, but the rewards can make the effort worthwhile.

### 3. Set Yearly, Monthly, and Weekly Goals

A million-dollar goal is achievable when broken down into incremental financial targets. Setting yearly, monthly, and even weekly goals helps you stay accountable and maintain focus.

Carlos, a marketing consultant, set an ambitious yearly goal of saving $50,000. To keep himself on track, he divided this into monthly savings goals of approximately $4,200. Each week, he reviewed his finances, tracking both income and expenses. Having short-term goals helped him stay disciplined, and over the years, he saw his net worth grow consistently toward his million-dollar target.

By tracking progress in smaller increments, Carlos stayed motivated and had a clear roadmap to reach his ultimate goal. This approach allowed him to make adjustments whenever he fell behind and gave him the flexibility to stay on course.

Setting realistic goals and building a wealth mindset are foundational steps to reaching your first million. This journey involves more than hitting a financial target; it's about transforming your thinking, building resilience, and developing the habits that will sustain long-term wealth.

By learning to break down large goals, cultivate patience, and invest in both skills and income diversity, you'll set yourself up for a path of growth and opportunity. People who have successfully reached their first million, like Sarah, Tom, Elena, Raj, Lily, and Josh, all started with realistic, actionable steps and a strong belief in their own potential. These are lessons that can be applied by anyone willing to put in the effort, and they form the core of a lasting wealth-building strategy.

Every step you take, every goal you achieve, brings you one step closer to financial freedom and a mindset of abundance that will sustain your wealth long after your first million is in the bank.

The Role of Positive Habits, Discipline, and Consistency in Building Wealth

Achieving a million-dollar goal isn't just about making smart investments or finding high-paying opportunities; it's about creating and maintaining positive financial habits, exercising discipline in your choices, and consistently taking action over time. Together, these three factors help build a solid path to wealth that can withstand setbacks, market changes, and life's unexpected turns. Let's explore each one in depth.

1. Positive Habits: Building a Wealth Foundation through Daily Actions

Positive financial habits are the small, regular actions you take that, over time, have a compounding effect on your wealth. These habits become part of your daily routine, allowing you to make incremental progress toward financial goals without feeling overwhelmed.

## Automating Savings and Investments

One of the simplest yet most powerful habits for wealth-building is automating your savings and investments. When a portion of your income is automatically transferred to a savings or investment account, you're actively prioritising your financial future without having to think about it constantly. Automating this process also prevents overspending and ensures that you're regularly building wealth, even if it's in small amounts at first.

For example, Lisa, a teacher, automated 10% of her paycheque to be invested in a low-cost index fund. Although her initial contributions were modest, over time they grew significantly thanks to the power of compounding. By the time she reached her 10-year milestone, her investments had grown substantially, and she was well on her way to her million-dollar goal - all because she made saving a habit that required minimal effort.

Tracking Expenses and Practicing Mindful Spending

A crucial habit for wealth-building is mindful spending. This means consciously evaluating where your money goes and cutting out unnecessary expenses. When you're aware of your spending habits, you're better able to allocate funds toward things that truly matter, such as savings, investments, or skills that increase your income potential.

Ben, a recent college graduate, found himself struggling with impulse spending. By tracking his expenses daily and reflecting on his spending patterns, he became more intentional about his purchases. Over time, he realized that he could save an additional $500 each month by cutting out nonessential spending, bringing him closer to his financial goals faster. This habit of mindful spending allowed him to focus his money on what would support his future.

2. Discipline: Making Sacrifices Today for Financial Freedom Tomorrow

Discipline is the mental and emotional strength to make sacrifices and delay gratification for long-term financial benefits. When you have financial discipline, you're better equipped to resist spending on short-term luxuries and, instead, commit to actions that will benefit you in the future.

### Sticking to a Budget

Setting and sticking to a budget is one of the most effective ways to exercise financial discipline. A budget isn't about restriction; it's about giving you control over your money and ensuring it's directed toward your priorities.

Take Rachel, a small business owner who made a conscious decision to live on a strict budget despite increasing income from her business. By sticking to her budget, she was able to save 30% of her earnings, which she invested back into her business and a retirement account. This discipline not only helped Rachel grow her wealth but also gave her a strong sense of financial security, enabling her to reach her million-dollar goal sooner.

### Avoiding Unnecessary Debt

Another key aspect of financial discipline is resisting unnecessary debt. While some debt (like a mortgage or student loan) can be part of a sound financial strategy, consumer debt, like high-interest credit cards, can derail wealth-building efforts.

For instance, James, a recent graduate, made a habit of avoiding debt whenever possible. By living below his means and building an emergency fund, he managed to stay out of debt, which allowed him to put more money toward investments. This discipline of debt avoidance gave James financial flexibility and minimized the stress of interest payments, accelerating his journey toward wealth.

3. Consistency: The Power of Repeated Actions Over Time

Consistency is what separates those who achieve their financial goals from those who start but don't follow through. Wealth-building is a marathon, not a sprint, and the real magic happens when you stick to your positive habits and disciplined choices consistently over time.

The Compounding Effect of Small, Regular Investments

Small, regular contributions to savings or investments might not seem significant initially, but the power of compounding can transform modest sums into substantial wealth over time. When you're consistent with your investments, you allow compounding to work in your favor, building momentum that accelerates your progress.

For example, Alex, a nurse, started investing just $200 a month in her 20s. At first, it felt like a small drop in the bucket, but she committed to this routine every month. By her late 40s, Alex's consistent contributions had grown into a portfolio worth hundreds of thousands of dollars — a testament to the power of consistency and compounding. By sticking to her plan, Alex was able to reach her financial goals sooner than she'd imagined.

Setting Routine Financial Check-ins

Regularly reviewing your financial goals, budget, and progress is another practice that reinforces consistency. This can be a weekly, monthly, or quarterly habit where you assess where you stand and make adjustments as needed.

Tom, a freelancer, sets aside an hour every Friday to review his earnings, expenses, and savings progress. This habit allows him to stay on top of his financial situation and make any necessary adjustments. Over time, these weekly check-ins have helped Tom stay motivated, disciplined, and aligned with his wealth-building goals. This habit of consistent financial review has been a powerful anchor, helping Tom make informed decisions and see consistent progress.

Why Positive Habits, Discipline, and Consistency Are Essential for Building Wealth

### 1. They Create a Strong Financial Foundation

Positive habits, discipline, and consistency build a stable foundation that enables you to handle both expected and unexpected financial situations. For instance, disciplined budgeting or automated saving becomes a "financial cushion," so you're less likely to be derailed by emergencies. By establishing a solid routine, you're also less vulnerable to impulsive decisions that might harm your financial health.

### 2. They Foster Resilience and Patience

Building wealth is a long-term commitment, and setbacks are inevitable. With discipline, positive habits, and consistency, you're more resilient in the face of these setbacks. Rather than giving up, you have the patience and strength to persevere, knowing that your efforts will pay off over time. These qualities make it easier to stay the course, even when the path to a million dollars feels slow or uncertain.

### 3. They Create a Compounding Effect on Wealth and Skills

Consistency and discipline don't only apply to money; they also apply to building skills and increasing your income potential. As you build positive financial habits and stay disciplined in your spending, saving, and investing, you also start accumulating knowledge and skills that amplify your earning potential. This compounding effect extends beyond money, creating lasting benefits that contribute to your wealth and personal growth.

## Building Wealth One Habit at a Time

Achieving a million dollars isn't necessarily about massive leaps or sudden windfalls; it's about a gradual, intentional build-up of positive habits, disciplined choices, and consistent actions. Each habit you create, each act of discipline, and each consistent step brings you closer to your financial goals. The true power of these elements lies in their compounding effect, as they strengthen and support each other, allowing your wealth to grow steadily over time.

So, as you set out on your journey toward financial freedom, remember that the daily habits you cultivate, the disciplined choices you make, and the consistent effort you put in will form the bedrock of your success. It's a path that requires patience and perseverance but ultimately leads to lasting wealth and financial security.

Developing Resilience to Overcome Setbacks on Your Path to Wealth

Building wealth is rarely a smooth journey. The path to achieving your first million will likely involve obstacles, unexpected expenses, market downturns, and personal challenges. Resilience, the ability to bounce back and continue pushing forward despite these setbacks, is crucial for anyone aiming to build long-term wealth. Resilience isn't just about enduring tough times—it's about adapting, learning, and growing stronger from each challenge you encounter. In this section, we'll look at how you can develop resilience to keep moving forward on your financial journey, no matter what life throws at you.

## 1. Recognizing Setbacks as Learning Opportunities

Resilient people view setbacks as temporary challenges and opportunities for growth rather than permanent roadblocks. When you shift your perspective to see setbacks as chances to learn, it becomes easier to stay motivated and keep moving toward your goals. This mindset change can help you not only recover from setbacks but also emerge stronger and better prepared for future challenges.

Take Emma, a young entrepreneur who launched her first online business. Shortly after launching, she encountered technical issues, a lack of customers, and higher expenses than anticipated. Instead of giving up, she viewed each of these setbacks as a learning opportunity. By examining what went wrong, she learned to optimize her website, improve her marketing strategy, and streamline her expenses. Within a year, her business was thriving, thanks to her ability to learn from her initial struggles. Emma's resilience transformed her setbacks into stepping stones toward her million-dollar goal.

2. Building an Emergency Fund to Provide Financial Cushion

One of the most practical ways to build resilience is to establish an emergency fund. An emergency fund is a dedicated savings account meant to cover unexpected expenses, like medical bills, car repairs, or job loss. Having an emergency fund can relieve some of the stress associated with financial setbacks, allowing you to address issues without derailing your long-term goals.

For example, James, a software engineer, built up an emergency fund with six months' worth of living expenses. When he unexpectedly lost his job, this fund provided him with a financial cushion, allowing him to focus on finding the right new position rather than taking the first available job out of necessity. His emergency fund served as a resilience tool, helping him stay on track without having to tap into his investments or go into debt.

Setting aside even a small percentage of your income regularly for an emergency fund builds resilience, enabling you to face challenges with confidence and protect your wealth-building progress.

### 3. Practicing Mental Flexibility and Adaptability

Financial resilience isn't just about money—it's also about mental flexibility and the ability to adapt when plans don't go as expected. In a constantly changing economic landscape, having a rigid mindset can be a major obstacle. Those who succeed in building wealth often adapt to changing conditions, exploring new strategies and making adjustments based on what's happening around them.

Carlos, for instance, was heavily invested in one sector of the stock market. When that sector took a downturn, instead of panicking or holding on to a failing strategy, he diversified his investments. This adaptability allowed him to recover from his losses and rebuild his portfolio with a more resilient and balanced approach. Carlos's experience taught him the importance of staying flexible and embracing change as a part of his wealth-building journey.

Building resilience involves cultivating a mindset that's open to change. This adaptability allows you to stay calm and look for new opportunities, even during challenging times.

4. Developing a Growth Mindset for Lifelong Learning

A growth mindset—the belief that abilities and intelligence can be developed over time—is an essential part of resilience. When you approach your financial journey with a growth mindset, you become more resilient because you see each experience, good or bad, as an opportunity to learn and grow. This mindset helps you stay focused on improvement rather than perfection, which is crucial in wealth-building.

Consider Maya, who wanted to increase her income but had no formal business training. She faced several failed ventures in her first few years, but each setback pushed her to acquire new skills in digital marketing, negotiation, and financial management. Maya's growth mindset made her resilient; each failure was a chance to become better equipped for her next venture. Eventually, her persistence paid off when she launched a successful consulting business, proving that resilience and a commitment to learning are vital to building wealth.

By continuously seeking out learning opportunities and refusing to let setbacks define you, a growth mindset keeps you resilient and forward-focused.

5. Building a Support System to Help You Stay Motivated

Resilience can be strengthened by the people you surround yourself with. Having a supportive network—whether it's friends, family, mentors, or a professional community—provides encouragement and perspective, helping you navigate setbacks without feeling isolated.

Sara, a real estate investor, encountered numerous challenges early on, including a failed property deal and a costly renovation. During these times, her mentor helped her analyze what went wrong and encouraged her to keep going. By learning from someone who had already achieved her financial goals, Sara gained valuable insights and avoided mistakes that could have cost her more in the future. Her support system gave her both the guidance and emotional resilience to persist and succeed.

Building a network of supportive individuals who share your goals or have expertise in areas you're working on can give you a psychological boost and practical advice, making it easier to stay resilient through challenges.

6. Setting Realistic Expectations and Celebrating Small Wins

Setting realistic expectations is crucial for resilience because it helps you avoid discouragement when things don't progress as quickly as you'd hoped. Wealth-building is a long-term commitment, and setting small, incremental goals along the way can keep you motivated and focused on the journey.

Ethan, who was working to pay off debt while saving for his first rental property, initially found it difficult to stay motivated. To help maintain his focus, he set small, realistic goals each month, like saving $500 or making an extra debt payment. He also celebrated each milestone, no matter how small. This approach kept him motivated, helping him build the resilience to stay on track even when the process felt slow.

By recognizing and celebrating each step forward, you reinforce your progress and build the mental resilience needed to pursue bigger financial goals.

7. Embracing Setbacks as Part of the Process

Finally, developing resilience means embracing setbacks as a natural part of the wealth-building process. In any journey, there will be highs and lows, moments of progress, and times of regression. Recognizing that setbacks are not failures but integral parts of the process can prevent discouragement and burnout.

Linda, a freelance writer, experienced a period of low income during an economic downturn. Rather than viewing this setback as a failure, she saw it as an opportunity to diversify her income streams. She took on additional skills, like content marketing and SEO, which allowed her to offer new services. Her ability to see the setback as a stepping stone rather than a dead end allowed her to bounce back stronger and more capable.

By embracing setbacks as temporary challenges, you shift your focus from what went wrong to what you can do to improve, allowing you to build resilience and continue progressing.

Building Resilience for Long-Term Wealth

Resilience is not a single trait but a collection of mindsets and practices that empower you to overcome challenges, adapt to new situations, and continue moving forward on your financial journey. By embracing setbacks, cultivating a growth mindset, building a support system, and celebrating small wins, you can develop the resilience to face any obstacle that arises.

Each setback you encounter and each lesson you learn contributes to your ability to navigate life's challenges with confidence. Building wealth requires persistence and resilience, and each time you overcome an obstacle, you reinforce your commitment to your goals. With resilience, setbacks become less intimidating, your vision remains clear, and the path to your first million becomes achievable.

# CHAPTER 3

## Mastering Income Streams – Exploring and Choosing the Right Income Streams

Earning your first million often requires more than just a single job or income source. Many successful millionaires diversify their income streams, balancing active and passive sources to accelerate their wealth-building efforts and increase financial security. Mastering income streams means understanding the range of ways you can earn money and finding a balance that fits your lifestyle, skills, and long-term goals.

In this chapter, we'll explore the difference between active and passive income, provide guidance on how to choose income streams that align with your personal strengths, and share stories of individuals who built wealth by creating a mix of income sources. By understanding the different avenues available to you and strategically diversifying your income, you can make the journey to financial freedom faster, more stable, and more fulfilling.

The Foundation of Income Streams: Active vs. Passive Income

Before diving into specific income streams, it's essential to understand the difference between active and passive income. Each type has unique advantages, challenges, and contributions to your overall financial picture.

## Active Income: Trading Time for Money

Active income refers to money earned by actively working or providing services. This includes traditional employment, freelancing, consulting, and even side hustles like delivering goods or offering online tutoring. In general, active income requires a direct investment of time and effort, and you're paid based on the work you do.

Consider Alex, a software engineer who earns a high salary but relies solely on his job as his main source of income. While his position provides a stable and consistent pay-check, he realises that if he were to stop working, his income would also stop. This reliance on active income limits Alex's financial freedom, as he's bound by the hours he works. He begins exploring ways to build passive income streams to create a more secure and diversified financial base.

Active income often forms the foundation of wealth-building, especially in the beginning stages, as it provides immediate cash flow that can be invested into other ventures. However, relying solely on active income has limitations, as it ties your earning potential directly to your available time.

## Passive Income: Earning Money While You Sleep

Passive income is money earned with minimal ongoing effort after an initial investment of time, money, or both. Once set up, passive income streams can continue to generate cash flow with little additional input, making them a powerful tool for long-term wealth building. Examples of passive income include rental properties, dividend-yielding stocks, royalties from books or music, and online businesses.

Take Samantha, who spent several years creating a popular online course about graphic design. After investing time upfront to develop, market, and refine the course, she now earns a steady stream of income from students who sign up each month. Though Samantha occasionally updates her material, most of the work has already been done, allowing her to earn money even while she focuses on other projects.

The main appeal of passive income is its ability to free up your time while still generating money, giving you the flexibility to explore new ventures or simply enjoy more time for yourself. However, passive income streams often require substantial effort, investment, or risk upfront, making it important to choose those that align with your financial goals and risk tolerance.

Choosing the Right Mix: Creating a Balanced Portfolio of Income Streams

For most people, the path to financial freedom isn't about choosing active or passive income exclusively; it's about finding a balance between the two. Your financial goals, risk tolerance, and available time will help determine the right mix of income streams for you. A balanced portfolio can help provide immediate cash flow, security, and long-term growth potential.

1. Starting with Your Strengths and Skills

When exploring income streams, it's often best to start with what you already know. Your current skills, professional background, and interests can inform the types of active or passive income streams you pursue. Leveraging your strengths allows you to build income sources faster and with a lower learning curve, which can accelerate your journey to wealth.

For example, Raj, an accountant, decided to use his financial expertise to offer freelance consulting services to small businesses. As he gained clients and became more efficient with his processes, he expanded his business to include online courses on financial literacy and small business accounting. By starting with his strengths, **Raj** was able to build active income from consulting and passive income from course sales, creating a balanced income portfolio that maximised his skills and minimised his initial investment.

2. Active Income Streams: Building Blocks of Wealth

While many dream of passive income, active income is often the starting point for building wealth. Active income provides the cash flow necessary for living expenses, investments, and building passive income streams. Let's explore some of the main ways people can build active income streams.

Employment and Side Hustles

For most people, a traditional job is the first step in building wealth. It provides stable income, benefits, and a reliable way to support daily expenses. However, a single job alone may not be enough to reach your financial goals, especially if you're aiming for a million-dollar net worth. Side hustles, freelancing, and consulting are excellent ways to increase active income without giving up the security of a full-time job.

Consider Monica, a marketing professional who decided to freelance on weekends to supplement her income. She used her expertise to take on short-term marketing projects and even started a small social media management agency with a few clients. By diversifying her active income, Monica accelerated her savings and increased her ability to invest in passive income opportunities.

Commission-Based and Performance-Based Income

If you're in sales, real estate, or any field that rewards performance, you may be able to significantly increase your income through commissions. Performance-based income can be lucrative, as it rewards results rather than time spent. It also incentivises skill-building and performance improvement, which can further boost your earning potential.

Lucas, a real estate agent, earns a base salary but has the potential to earn large commissions for each sale he closes. He has taken advantage of this structure by specializing in luxury properties, which has higher commission rates. Lucas's income varies month-to-month, but the high earning potential has allowed him to save and invest aggressively, building a foundation that he later leverages for passive income.

3. Passive Income Streams: Creating a Path to Financial Independence

While active income is the starting point, passive income provides the freedom and flexibility that many aspire to. Let's explore some popular passive income streams and how they can contribute to your wealth-building strategy.

Real Estate Investments

Real estate is one of the most popular forms of passive income because it provides cash flow, tax benefits, and long-term appreciation. Investing in rental properties, commercial spaces, or even real estate investment trusts (REITs) can generate ongoing income with minimal day-to-day involvement.

Eva, a nurse, saved up enough to purchase her first rental property in a growing area. She hires a property manager to handle tenant issues, allowing her to earn rental income without actively managing the property. Over time, the property appreciates in value, and Eva uses the cash flow to reinvest in additional properties. Real estate becomes a cornerstone of her passive income, giving her the financial freedom to reduce her hours at work and focus on further investments.

Dividend Stocks and Index Funds

Investing in dividend stocks and index funds allows you to earn passive income through dividends, while also benefiting from long-term market appreciation.

Dividend stocks pay out a portion of the company's profits to shareholders, while index funds spread investments across various companies, reducing risk.

Chris, a graphic designer, began investing a portion of his income in dividend-paying stocks. Over time, his investments grow, and the dividends provide a steady income stream. By reinvesting his dividends, Chris can accelerate the growth of his portfolio, steadily increasing his passive income potential. This approach enables him to build wealth without requiring extensive management or trading knowledge.

Royalties and Licensing

If you're a creative professional or have specialised knowledge, royalties and licensing can be lucrative passive income sources. Authors, musicians, artists, and inventors earn royalties for their work, while licensing involves renting out intellectual property to others for use.

Lily, an author, published a book on career development and negotiated a royalty agreement with her publisher. Her book's popularity has led to a steady stream of royalty payments. Lily's initial effort in writing and promoting her book created an income source that continues to pay her for years, allowing her to focus on other projects while still earning money.

## Creating Digital Products or Online Courses

With the rise of digital platforms, creating and selling online courses, e-books, and other digital products has become an accessible form of passive income. Once created, digital products require minimal upkeep and can generate income indefinitely.

Marco, a web developer, created an online course on building websites. After spending a few months recording and editing his course, he launched it on a popular e-learning platform. The course sells consistently, generating a steady stream of income. Marco now has the flexibility to pursue other projects, knowing that his digital product continues to earn him passive income.

## 4. Diversifying Income Streams: Creating Financial Stability

While building wealth, relying on a single income source can be risky. Diversification spreads risk across different income streams, making your financial situation more resilient to unexpected events like job loss or market downturns. A combination of active and passive income streams provides immediate cash flow, long-term growth, and security.

Michael, an IT consultant, balances active income from consulting with passive income from rental properties and dividend stocks. This mix allows him to earn money regardless of market conditions or changes in his consulting workload. By diversifying, Michael not only increases his income but also minimises his risk, allowing him to pursue new opportunities with confidence.

## 5. Managing and Scaling Your Income Streams

Once you have multiple income streams, managing and scaling them becomes essential. This means periodically reviewing each source, rein

vesting profits, and optimising processes for maximum efficiency. Scaling your income streams allows you to increase your earnings without proportionately increasing your time investment.

Mastering income streams is about more than just earning more money; it's about creating a roadmap to financial independence. By choosing the right combination of active and passive income sources, you can accelerate your wealth-building journey and enjoy greater flexibility and security along the way.

As you work toward your first million, diversifying your income gives you control over your financial destiny, helping you stay resilient through life's ups and downs. By embracing the full range of income opportunities and building a portfolio that aligns with your strengths and goals, you'll create a solid foundation that will support you well beyond your first million.

Building a High-Income Skill Set: The Key to Unlocking Financial Opportunities

In today's rapidly evolving economy, possessing a high-income skill set can be one of the most effective ways to accelerate your journey to financial freedom. High-income skills are specialized abilities that are in high demand, can command premium pay, and often allow you to work in flexible roles or even become your own boss. Examples of these skills include sales, coding, digital marketing, copywriting, and public speaking. By developing one or more of these skills, you can increase your earning potential, create multiple streams of income, and ultimately fast-track your path to making your first million.

This section delves into the importance of high-income skills, how to choose the right ones, and real-world examples of people who have used high-income skills to transform their lives and finances.

## 1. Understanding the Value of High-Income Skills

High-income skills are valuable because they are both in demand and scalable. They go beyond entry-level knowledge, making you more attractive to employers or clients willing to pay a premium for your expertise. In many cases, these skills can also allow you to transition to freelance or consulting work, providing greater control over your schedule and income.

Take Nina, a marketing executive, for example. She decided to enhance her digital marketing knowledge by specialising in search engine optimisation (SEO). As she honed her skills, she began taking on freelance clients on the side, charging upwards of $150 per hour. Nina eventually built a client base that paid her more than her full-time job. With her high-income skill in SEO, she eventually launched her own agency, quadrupling her income within a few years.

Nina's story illustrates how high-income skills create financial leverage. Unlike traditional hourly work, high-income skills increase your earning potential without requiring an endless trade of time for money. Once you gain expertise in a high-income skill, you can command higher rates, work on high-profile projects, or scale your services to reach more clients and customers.

## 2. Choosing the Right High-Income Skill for You

With so many high-income skills to choose from, it's essential to select one that aligns with your interests, strengths, and market demand. Skills like coding, digital marketing, and sales are often in high demand, but the best skill for you will depend on your goals and preferred industry.

Here's a breakdown of a few popular high-income skills and what makes them valuable:

- Sales: Sales skills are foundational to virtually every industry. If you can sell—whether it's products, services, or ideas—you'll always have opportunities to make money. Sales skills also translate well into entrepreneurship, as selling is crucial for launching and growing any business. Mark, a real estate agent, learned advanced sales techniques and was able to increase his income through larger commissions on luxury properties, eventually becoming a top seller in his city.

- Coding: Coding is a versatile skill that's in high demand across tech and non-tech industries alike. Knowledge of programming languages like Python, JavaScript, and Ruby can open doors to high-paying software engineering jobs, freelance opportunities, and even the creation of software products or apps. Sarah, for instance, started as a junior developer, but her specialisation in backend development allowed her to command high salaries and eventually become a freelance consultant, earning twice as much.

- Digital Marketing: In the digital age, companies need experts who can help them reach customers online. Digital marketing covers a broad range of sub-skills, including SEO, social media marketing, content marketing, and email marketing. Developing expertise in one of these areas can make you invaluable to companies seeking to expand their online presence. Carlos, who specialised in social media marketing, initially worked for a digital agency but quickly began freelancing, helping small businesses grow their online followings. His success allowed him to establish a lucrative business managing multiple clients.

When choosing a high-income skill, research industry trends and determine where demand is strongest. You'll also want to consider your current abilities and whether you're willing to invest time and resources into building expertise.

3. How to Develop a High-Income Skill

Building a high-income skill isn't typically something that happens overnight; it requires dedication, practice, and often a substantial amount of learning. However, with the right approach, you can speed up the process and start earning sooner.

Here's a structured approach to developing a high-income skill:

1. Invest in Quality Education and Training: Start by taking high-quality courses, either online or in person. Many platforms, such as Udemy, Coursera, or LinkedIn Learning, offer affordable, structured courses taught by industry professionals. For instance, if you're interested in digital marketing, you might take a comprehensive course that covers everything from Google Ads to SEO to social media management.

2. Practice Consistently: Real expertise comes from hands-on experience. If you're learning coding, for example, start building projects as soon as possible, even if they're simple ones. If your focus is sales, seek out opportunities to apply your skills, whether through volunteer work, a part-time job, or even creating a sales-focused side hustle.

3. Network with Other Professionals: Surrounding yourself with people who excel in your chosen skill area can be incredibly valuable. By networking, you can gain insights, get feedback on your work, and even find mentors who can guide you. Industry events,

online forums, LinkedIn groups, and even local meetups can be great places to connect.

4. Seek Mentorship and Feedback: Mentors can provide invaluable feedback, guiding you through challenges and offering advice on building your career. Feedback can also come from clients, customers, or colleagues—be open to constructive criticism to continuously improve.

5. Stay Updated and Evolve: Industries are constantly changing, especially in fields like technology and digital marketing. Commit to continuous learning, so your skill remains relevant and in demand. Attending workshops, enrolling in advanced courses, or participating in professional groups can help keep you at the top of your field.

Emma, a copywriter, followed this approach by constantly seeking feedback from her clients and mentors. Her dedication to improvement led her to specialise in high-converting email marketing. As she refined her skills, she was able to triple her rates and attract larger clients, proving the value of focused, continuous skill development.

## 4. Leveraging High-Income Skills for Multiple Streams of Income

High-income skills often provide opportunities to diversify income. For example, a skilled coder can offer freelance services, create software products, teach coding, or even build and sell apps. High-income skills are not limited to a single job or employer—they allow for flexibility and multiple income streams.

Take Ben, a graphic designer. By honing his expertise in user experience (UX) design, he began freelancing for tech startups and soon had enough clients to quit his full-time job. Later, he developed an online course to teach others about UX, creating an additional passive income stream. Now, Ben's diversified income sources allow him to enjoy greater financial security and flexibility.

Some common ways to diversify income with high-income skills include:

- Consulting or Freelancing: Offering your services on a freelance basis allows you to work with various clients, set your rates, and control your workload.

- Teaching or Coaching: If you have expertise in a high-income skill, others are likely willing to pay to learn from you. Online courses, workshops, and one-on-one coaching can be lucrative options.

- Creating Digital Products: Many high-income skills lend themselves to creating valuable digital products, such as templates, software, or e-books.

- Building a Business: If your high-income skill is in demand, you may even consider building a business around it. Whether it's a digital agency, software company, or consultancy, turning your skill into a business can multiply your earning potential.

## 5. Real-Life Examples of Wealth Built with High-Income Skills

Success stories of people who have achieved financial freedom by leveraging high-income skills can be both inspiring and instructive.

Elena, a data analyst, specialised in machine learning, a high-demand skill that few people master. Initially, she worked in a corporate role but later transitioned to consulting for companies that needed her expertise. Eventually, she built a team and founded her own data consulting firm, which now brings in six figures annually. By focusing on a specialised, high-income skill, Elena was able to achieve financial independence and create wealth.

Another example is John, who started as a salesperson in a corporate setting. John spent years refining his sales techniques, investing time in books, seminars, and networking events. He developed expertise in high-stakes negotiation and later transitioned to freelance sales consulting. Today, he works with tech startups, helping them close major deals and earning a percentage of each sale. His high-income skill in sales enabled him to become financially independent and build wealth through consulting and performance-based income.

Developing a high-income skill is one of the smartest investments you can make on your journey to financial freedom. These skills not only increase your earning potential but also offer opportunities for flexible, scalable income that can support your long-term financial goals. By choosing a skill that aligns with your strengths, dedicating yourself to continuous learning, and leveraging your expertise to create multiple income streams, you can accelerate your journey to your first million and build a solid foundation for a lifetime of financial independence.

Mastering a high-income skill is about more than just acquiring knowledge; it's about creating new opportunities, increasing your value, and ultimately, taking control of your financial future. Whether through coding, sales, digital marketing, or another skill, building expertise will empower you to build wealth in ways that few other pursuits can match.

Maximising Your Primary Income While Creating Additional Streams: Laying a Strong Foundation for Financial Freedom

When building toward your first million, the most reliable foundation is often your primary income source. For many, this is their day job or main business

— something they're deeply invested in and that forms the bulk of their current earnings. Maximising your primary income allows you to build capital, develop expertise, and establish financial stability. However, relying solely on one income source is rarely sufficient for long-term financial independence. Creating additional income streams, whether through side hustles, investments, or passive income channels, is key to accelerating wealth accumulation.

In this section, we'll explore strategies for maximising your primary income while diversifying through other revenue streams, along with real-world examples to illustrate how these principles can be applied in your financial journey.

1. Maximising Your Primary Income

Maximising your primary income doesn't just mean earning more; it means strategically positioning yourself to leverage every opportunity for growth within your main source of income. Whether you're an employee or a business owner, here are several ways to maximise your primary income:

- Seek Promotions or Raises: As an employee, demonstrating value and advocating for raises can significantly impact your income. Look for ways to take on additional responsibilities, expand your skill set, and deliver consistently high performance. When you bring quantifiable results, such as increased sales, reduced costs, or improved processes, you can make a strong case for a raise or promotion.

- Negotiate Your Salary: Salary negotiation is a crucial skill for maximising income. Research the market rates for your role, understand the value you bring, and don't be afraid to negotiate. Sometimes, switching companies can lead to a significant pay increase, especially if your industry's demand for skilled professionals is high.

- Invest in Skill Development: Continual learning can lead to greater earning potential. High-income skills, as mentioned earlier, make you more valuable and open doors to higher-paying positions. If you're a software developer, for instance, specialising in a niche technology can make you indispensable to certain employers, allowing you to command a premium rate.

- Expand Your Business: If you own a business, look for opportunities to scale. This could involve expanding your product line, entering new markets, or streamlining operations to increase profitability. By optimising your main source of income, you can create a financial base that makes it easier to pursue additional revenue streams.

- Develop a Reputation as an Expert: Becoming known as an expert in your field can lead to consulting opportunities, speaking engagements, and other income-generating roles. As you build a reputation, you may find opportunities to earn extra income or even transition to a higher-paying position.

Example: Mike, a corporate attorney, maximised his primary income by specialising in intellectual property law. By becoming a thought leader, he was invited to speak at conferences and consult for high-profile clients, significantly increasing his annual income.

2. Using Your Primary Income as a Launchpad for Additional Streams

Once you've maximised your primary income, you're in a stronger position to invest in other opportunities. Here's how you can use your primary income as a springboard for creating additional revenue streams:

- Automate Savings for Investments: Set aside a fixed portion of your income to invest in other streams. Automating your savings ensures you're consistently building a financial reserve without manually managing it. This reserve can then be used to fund ventures such as real estate, stocks, or other investment opportunities.

- Invest in Real Estate: Real estate remains one of the most popular and profitable ways to generate passive income. By saving up from your primary income, you can make down payments on rental properties, which generate regular cash flow. Additionally, real estate investments often appreciate, adding to your wealth over time.

- Start a Side Business: Many professionals turn hobbies or interests into side businesses that complement their primary income. If you're a graphic designer, for instance, you could start freelancing on the side. A side business is particularly valuable if it aligns with your skills, as it requires less time and training to launch.

- Develop Passive Income Streams: Use your primary income to fund passive income sources, such as dividends from stocks, rental properties, or royalties from creative work. With enough capital, you can buy into investments that pay dividends, bonds, or REITs (Real Estate Investment Trusts), which offer regular income with minimal maintenance.

Example: Sarah, a high school teacher, used her salary to buy her first rental property. She then reinvested her rental income to purchase additional properties, building a portfolio that generated significant passive income.

## 3. Creating Complementary Income Streams

One of the most effective ways to build wealth is to create income streams that are complementary to your primary income. These streams not only supplement your earnings but also align with your expertise, reducing the time and effort needed to establish them.

- Freelancing in Your Field: Leveraging your primary skills in a freelance or consulting capacity can provide additional income while reinforcing your main job's expertise. For instance, if you're a software developer, taking on freelance projects can increase your earnings and broaden your network, leading to new opportunities.

- Teaching or Coaching: If you're an expert in a high-demand field, teaching or coaching can be a lucrative income stream. Platforms like Udemy or Skillshare allow you to create online courses that generate passive income, while one-on-one coaching can provide a more hands-on revenue stream. Teaching others can also deepen your own knowledge and position you as an authority in your industry.

- Royalties from Intellectual Property: If you have a creative skill, consider developing intellectual property that generates royalties, such as books, music, or art. Royalties provide ongoing revenue after the initial work is completed and can be a substantial income stream if your work becomes popular.

Example: Jared, an accountant, began creating online courses to help small business owners manage their finances. His expertise made him a popular instructor, and the course royalties provided consistent, passive income over time.

4. Diversifying with Investments

Investing is a powerful way to diversify your income streams, and maximising your primary income gives you the financial freedom to make investments that align with your goals. Here are several ways to invest and diversify income:

- Stock Market Investments: Investing in stocks is one of the simplest ways to diversify income. You can choose dividend-paying stocks that provide regular income or growth stocks that appreciate over time. The stock market offers a range of options to suit different risk tolerances and financial goals.

- Real Estate Investments: Beyond rental properties, real estate offers other opportunities, such as REITs and real estate crowdfunding, which provide access to property income with lower capital requirements. Rental income from properties, coupled with property appreciation, makes real estate a versatile way to build wealth.

- Peer-to-Peer Lending: Peer-to-peer lending allows you to lend money directly to individuals or small businesses in exchange for interest payments. While riskier than traditional investments, it can provide high returns, making it an option for those seeking to diversify.

Example: Emily, a financial analyst, used her salary to buy dividend stocks, real estate, and even some bonds, diversifying her portfolio and creating a steady income that supplemented her primary income from work.

5. Managing and Balancing Multiple Income Streams

Creating multiple income streams requires balancing time, energy, and resources to avoid burnout. Start by focusing on maximising your primary income, then add new streams gradually. It's essential to prioritise quality over quantity; a few high-performing income streams are often more effective than juggling many low-yield options.

Here are some tips for managing multiple income streams:

- Automate Wherever Possible: Automating savings, investments, or even parts of a side business can reduce the time you spend managing these streams.

- Monitor and Reinvest: Regularly assess the performance of each income stream. Reinvesting the profits from one stream into another, such as using side business earnings to fund stock investments, can accelerate your wealth-building process.

- Set Time Limits for Each Stream: Allocate specific hours per week or month to manage your income streams, and be strict with these boundaries. Time management is crucial to prevent your side ventures from interfering with your primary income source.

Maximising your primary income while developing additional income streams is a powerful strategy for accelerating your journey to financial freedom. Each income stream not only supplements your earnings but also provides financial security, cushioning you against market shifts and career uncertainties. By taking a balanced approach and investing strategically, you'll create a robust financial foundation that paves the way for long-term wealth.

Whether it's through advancing in your career, freelancing, investing, or building passive income, the goal is to increase your financial resilience and multiply your income streams. This strategic diversification will empower you to build wealth faster and with greater stability, setting you up not just to earn your first million but to enjoy the security and freedom that comes with sustained financial independence.

# CHAPTER 4

Smart Savings Strategies – Budgeting Basics: How to Save Without Sacrificing Quality of Life

When people think about saving money, they often imagine a life of restriction, sacrificing small joys, and adopting a frugal lifestyle. But true financial freedom doesn't mean giving up what you enjoy; rather, it's about prioritising what matters most to you and aligning your spending to support those priorities. Smart saving is not about depriving yourself—it's about learning to use your money in a way that enriches your life, helps you build wealth, and sets you up for future success.

In this chapter, we'll explore the fundamentals of budgeting, shifting from a scarcity mindset to an abundance mindset, and practical strategies to maximise your savings while enjoying life. This journey toward smarter savings is filled with insights, real-world stories, and strategies that show how small changes in your financial habits can lead to substantial gains without feeling like a sacrifice.

## 1. The Foundation of Smart Savings: Understanding Your Relationship with Money

Before diving into specific budgeting techniques, let's start with the mindset that underpins smart savings. Think of budgeting not as a restrictive practice, but as a method for gaining control over your finances. To do this, it's essential to evaluate your relationship with money.

Take Jake, for example, a young professional who grew up in a household where money was tight. He was taught that saving meant cutting back on everything, from dining out to skipping vacations, which led him to associate budgeting with feelings of restriction. But when Jake started working with a financial coach, he learned that budgeting didn't have to mean depriving himself. Instead, he was encouraged to identify what truly mattered to him and build a spending plan around those values.

By reframing his relationship with money, Jake found he could still enjoy dining out, taking occasional trips, and even indulging in a monthly spa day—because he was intentional about where his money went. The shift from seeing budgeting as a constraint to viewing it as a tool for empowerment made a significant difference. He realised he wasn't giving things up; he was creating a plan that allowed him to enjoy life now while securing his future.

2. Setting the Ground Rules: The Basics of Budgeting

The foundation of a successful budget is knowing where your money goes. This doesn't mean tracking every penny, but it does mean having a clear understanding of your essential expenses, discretionary spending, and savings goals. A budget isn't just numbers on a page; it's a map that guides your financial journey, ensuring you're moving toward financial freedom without detours.

One of the most effective ways to start budgeting is to use the 50/30/20 Rule:

- 50% for Essentials: Rent, utilities, groceries, transportation, and other necessary expenses should take up no more than half of your income.

- 30% for Discretionary Spending: This category includes things like dining out, entertainment, travel, and hobbies. It's your "fun" money, allowing you to enjoy life without feeling guilty.

- 20% for Savings and Debt Repayment: The remaining portion should go toward building an emergency fund, saving for future goals, and paying down debt.

This rule isn't set in stone, but it provides a balanced framework that can be adjusted to suit your personal situation.

Example: Laura, a recent college graduate, was earning an entry-level salary and felt overwhelmed by student loans and credit card debt. Using the 50/30/20 Rule, she allocated her income and began to see where her money was going each month. Laura was surprised to find that small daily expenses—like $5 lattes and frequent dining out—added up quickly. By making a few adjustments and sticking to her budget, she freed up extra money to put toward her debt and savings, giving her a sense of accomplishment and progress.

3. Saving Smarter, Not Harder: Prioritising Quality of Life

Contrary to popular belief, budgeting doesn't have to strip your life of fun. The key to saving without sacrificing quality of life lies in identifying what truly matters to you and spending money on those things while cutting back on less important areas. This approach is sometimes referred to as "value-based spending."

Jenna had always loved travel, but with a modest salary, she felt like her dream of seeing the world was out of reach. After re-evaluating her spending, she realised that much of her discretionary spending went toward things she didn't actually enjoy that much— like nights out she felt obligated to attend or clothes she bought to keep up with trends. By cutting back in those areas, Jenna was able to save a travel fund and started taking budget-friendly trips twice a year. For her, the joy of travel far outweighed the sacrifice of skipping a few social events.

This approach—knowing what you value most and consciously choosing to spend money in those areas—can transform the way you save. It's not about "cutting back"; it's about choosing to invest in experiences, things, and goals that bring you genuine happiness.

4. Automating Your Savings: The Power of 'Paying Yourself First'

One of the most effective ways to build your savings without even thinking about it is by automating the process. The concept of "paying yourself first" involves setting up an automatic transfer to your savings account each time you receive your pay-check. This strategy ensures that you prioritise saving before you even have the chance to spend.

When Tim first heard about paying himself first, he was skeptical. Living pay-check to pay-check, he wasn't sure he could afford to save. But he decided to try automating just 5% of his income to a high-yield savings account. Over time, he increased this percentage to 10% and then 15% as he adjusted his spending. To his surprise, Tim barely noticed the difference in his daily life—but his savings grew steadily. By automating his savings, he created a financial buffer that made him feel secure and in control.

Automating savings isn't about making drastic cuts; it's about creating a habit that builds your wealth over time. When you treat saving as a non-negotiable part of your budget, you'll find it easier to grow your savings without feeling the pinch.

5. The Art of Frugal Fun: Enjoying Life on a Budget

One of the greatest misconceptions about budgeting is that it's boring and limits your ability to have fun. However, frugal living doesn't mean living without joy; it just means getting creative with how you spend. Many people discover that cutting back on expenses doesn't limit their quality of life—it can actually enhance it.

For example, Renee and Marcus, a couple with a shared love for fine dining, were trying to save for a down payment on a house. Rather than giving up their date nights, they decided to replicate their favourite restaurant meals at home. They turned cooking together into a weekly ritual, experimenting with new recipes and even hosting "dinner parties" where friends would bring ingredients to contribute.

This approach saved them hundreds of dollars a month and added a sense of excitement to their meals. They enjoyed the process so much that they continued even after reaching their savings goal.

From finding affordable events in your city to exploring nature trails, libraries, and local museums, there are countless ways to have fun without spending a lot. By finding alternatives to expensive activities, you can enjoy life to the fullest while still building your financial future.

6. Tracking Your Progress: Using Tools and Techniques to Stay on Track

Budgeting without tracking your progress is like setting out on a journey without checking the map. There are numerous tools, apps, and techniques you can use to monitor your spending and stay accountable to your goals.

Ashley, a young entrepreneur, found herself struggling with overspending. She started using a budgeting app to track her expenses in real-time. This gave her insight into her spending patterns and helped her make conscious choices about her money. Whenever she noticed she was approaching her budget limit in a certain category, she would pause and evaluate whether the purchase aligned with her goals.

Budgeting tools like Mint, YNAB (You Need A Budget), and even simple spreadsheets can be immensely helpful. By regularly reviewing your spending, you can catch bad habits early and adjust before they become larger issues. Tracking your budget also provides a sense of satisfaction as you watch your savings grow and see tangible progress toward your financial goals.

7. Preparing for Unexpected Expenses: Building an Emergency Fund

An essential part of smart saving is preparing for the unexpected. Life is full of surprises, and having an emergency fund ensures that unforeseen expenses don't derail your financial plan. Experts recommend having at least three to six months' worth of living expenses in an easily accessible account.

When David faced unexpected car repairs, he was grateful for his emergency fund. Instead of relying on credit cards or loans, he used his emergency fund to cover the cost, avoiding debt and maintaining his financial momentum. David's story is a reminder of the peace of mind an emergency fund can bring.

Building an emergency fund may seem daunting, but it doesn't have to happen overnight. Start by setting aside a small percentage of your income each month. Even if you can only contribute a small amount, consistency will help your fund grow over time, providing a safety net for life's uncertainties.

## 8. Planning for Future Goals: Saving with Purpose

Smart saving isn't just about cutting costs—it's about aligning your money with your dreams. Whether you're saving for a house, an education, or a dream vacation, having a clear purpose can make the process rewarding.

Emma, for example, wanted to start her own business. She set a specific savings goal and began setting aside money each month toward her "business fund." By visualising her goal and keeping it in focus, Emma was motivated to stick to her budget. She even created

a vision board as a reminder of what she was working toward, which helped her stay disciplined when she was tempted to splurge on unnecessary expenses.

Saving with purpose makes the journey meaningful and gives you a reason to stick to your plan. When you attach your budget to your long-term aspirations, you'll find it easier to make daily choices that align with your future.

Smart saving is not about deprivation; it's about choice, control, and intention. By following the budgeting basics and prioritising what you truly value, you can build a life where saving doesn't feel like a sacrifice. Small, consistent changes in your spending habits will gradually transform your financial landscape, bringing you closer to the goal of financial freedom.

The journey to your first million starts with mastering the art of budgeting, and this chapter has given you the tools to get started. From automating your savings to enjoying life on a budget, these strategies are designed to help you build wealth while living well.

Automating savings is one of the most effective and low-effort strategies for building wealth consistently over time. Unlike traditional saving methods, where you consciously decide to set money aside each month, automating savings removes the need for decision-making entirely. This approach leverages consistency and discipline, allowing you to grow your wealth without having to rely on motivation or the temptation to spend instead. It's a simple concept but has profound effects on your financial future.

Consider Brian's experience with automated savings. Brian was in his mid-twenties and, while he knew he should be saving, he often found himself spending any extra money he had left at the end of the month. He intended to save, but each time he looked at his bank account, there always seemed to be something else he wanted or needed. One day, a friend introduced him to the idea of automating his savings. Brian set up an automatic transfer, directing a portion of his paycheque to a savings account. He decided on a modest 10% to start. This money would go directly to his savings account as soon as he was paid, and since he never saw it in his checking account, he found it easy to forget it was even there.

Within a few months, Brian was surprised by how quickly his savings grew. The beauty of automating his savings was that he didn't feel like he was sacrificing his lifestyle. He had adjusted his spending habits, unconsciously aligning with his new, slightly smaller budget. After a year, Brian realized he'd saved more than he ever had before, simply by setting up that automatic transfer.

1. How Automation Builds Consistency
Automated savings work because they rely on the principle of paying yourself first. By arranging to have

a set percentage or fixed amount transferred to savings before you even have a chance to spend it, you ensure that your financial goals are prioritized. This method works on the psychology of inertia: it's easier to stick with an automatic process than to make saving decisions repeatedly. Once set, automated transfers happen in the background, creating a consistent growth in your savings without requiring ongoing effort.

Example: Consider an emergency fund, which financial experts suggest should hold at least three to six months of living expenses. Setting up an automated savings plan for this purpose means that you're gradually building this safety net each month. It becomes a non-negotiable part of your budget, and because it's automated, you don't have to feel like you're sacrificing anything to build this critical financial cushion.

## 2. Adopting a "Set It and Forget It" Mindset

The phrase "set it and forget it" perfectly captures the spirit of automated savings. Once you arrange a transfer to your savings or investment account, you don't need to give it a second thought. This method is particularly powerful for people who find it challenging to save consistently due to life's frequent expenses and surprises. By automating, you're ensuring that even on those months when extra costs come up or you feel tempted to overspend, your financial goals are still being met.

Example: Sarah, a young entrepreneur, wanted to invest in her retirement but felt overwhelmed by the process. Her financial advisor suggested she set up an automatic transfer to a retirement fund each month. Sarah set up an automatic transfer from her bank account to her Roth IRA and soon realized she had accumulated a significant amount without ever feeling the burden of setting aside funds manually.

3. Avoiding Temptation and Overspending

By automating your savings, you're effectively separating your "spendable" money from the money you intend to save. This separation has a powerful psychological effect: when your savings account is out of sight, you're less likely to dip into it for impulse purchases. Automation makes it feel as though the money set aside never existed in your daily budget, reducing the temptation to spend it on non-essential items.

Example: Dan loved eating out and frequently splurged on new gadgets. By the end of each month, he often found his checking account depleted, leaving little room for savings. After automating a monthly transfer to his savings account, Dan realized he no longer felt the urge to spend that money on impulse purchases. He gradually adjusted to his new budget, finding satisfaction in watching his savings grow rather than in short-lived purchases.

4. Building Wealth Through Compound Interest

Automated savings become even more powerful when you place those funds in an interest-bearing account or investment. Savings accounts, high-yield savings accounts, or even investment accounts like IRAs allow your money to grow over time, benefiting from compound interest. Compound interest, the process by which interest is earned on both the initial deposit and the accumulated interest, accelerates your savings growth over the long term. The earlier you start saving and automating those savings, the greater your compounding returns will be.

Example: Linda, in her early thirties, automated her savings into a high-yield savings account with an interest rate of 3%. Over the years, her contributions, combined with the interest accrued, grew her balance significantly. As her account balance grew, so did her interest, demonstrating the power of compound interest in building wealth.

5. Using Automation for Multiple Financial Goals

Automating savings isn't limited to a single account or purpose. Many people automate multiple transfers to cover various financial goals, such as retirement, emergency funds, travel funds, or even down payments on a house. By setting up different automated transfers for each goal, you can work toward several objectives simultaneously without feeling overwhelmed. Automating multiple savings streams also helps ensure you don't inadvertently neglect any financial goals in favor of others.

Example: Carlos had several financial goals: building an emergency fund, saving for a wedding, and contributing to a retirement account. He set up three automatic transfers from his checking account to different savings accounts designated for each goal. Every month, a portion of his paycheque went toward each of these accounts, making it easy for him to track his progress and stay motivated without having to allocate funds manually.

6. Steps to Start Automating Your Savings

If you're new to automating your savings, the process is simple and quick. Here's a step-by-step guide to get started:

- Identify a Target Amount: Decide on a comfortable percentage of your income to save. Start small if necessary and gradually increase it as you adjust.

- Choose the Right Accounts: Set up separate savings or investment accounts for each financial goal. High-yield accounts, retirement accounts, or even general savings accounts can be useful.

- Set a Frequency: Decide how often you'll transfer funds—this could be monthly, bi-weekly, or per paycheque.

- Automate the Transfer: Set up an automatic transfer from your checking account to your chosen savings account(s) through your bank's website or app.

- Review Periodically: Over time, check your progress and adjust your automated contributions as your financial situation changes.

## 7. The Psychological Rewards of Automation

When you automate your savings, you're not just building wealth; you're also building peace of mind. By making savings automatic, you reduce stress around finances, knowing that your future is being taken care of without requiring constant attention. This approach also helps cultivate a proactive mindset, as you're consistently taking steps toward financial freedom with minimal effort. Over time, you'll find that your confidence grows as your savings grow, creating a positive cycle of reinforcement.

Example: After Ava automated her savings, she noticed an unexpected benefit: she felt more relaxed and less anxious about money. Knowing that her savings were growing each month, even without constant monitoring, provided her with a deep sense of security. It allowed her to focus on other aspects of her life and career without worrying about whether she was saving enough.

Automating savings is a powerful strategy for consistent financial growth, offering numerous benefits beyond mere convenience. By putting your finances on autopilot, you can eliminate the mental load of saving, avoid the temptation of overspending, and benefit from compound interest—all while freeing up time and energy for other pursuits.

Automation turns saving into a seamless habit, allowing you to steadily build wealth without feeling the burden of constant budgeting and monitoring. For those on the journey toward their first million, automation is a simple yet profound tool that paves the way to financial independence, providing both immediate peace of mind and long-term financial security.

Cutting unnecessary expenses may sound like a tedious task, but when done with intention, it becomes a powerful tool for redirecting funds toward things that genuinely matter—goals that drive growth, opportunities for investment, and ultimately, financial freedom. This approach isn't about depriving yourself; rather, it's about freeing up money that would otherwise slip through the cracks and putting it to work for your future.

Take Nina's story, for example. In her late twenties and working in marketing, Nina earned a decent salary, yet her savings were barely growing. She felt like she was always busy, always spending, but at the end of each month, she was often left wondering where all her money had gone. She knew she wanted to save for her own business one day but couldn't figure out how to carve out the extra funds to make it happen.

Nina decided to try an expense audit. One weekend, she sat down and reviewed her bank and credit card statements from the past few months. She used different colored highlighters to mark her purchases—one color for essentials like rent and groceries, another for "comfort" purchases like coffee, and a third for big-ticket discretionary spending like clothes, beauty products, and dining out. By the time she finished highlighting, she was shocked at how much she'd spent on things that she couldn't even recall or that brought her only momentary happiness.

In her audit, Nina saw a pattern. She loved trying new restaurants, and her spending reflected that. But she also noticed how much she spent on quick lunches and coffee runs throughout the week. It wasn't that Nina couldn't afford to dine out occasionally; the issue was the frequency of smaller, seemingly insignificant purchases adding up. This awareness became a turning point for her.

1. Tackling Small, Daily Expenses: A Focus on Conscious Spending

Nina's first step was to limit her coffee runs to once a week. She also started meal-prepping on Sundays, which allowed her to bring lunch to work rather than grabbing something on the go. To make her new habits feel special, she invested in a high-quality thermos and a set of attractive meal containers. She found she actually looked forward to her weekly "treat" coffee and enjoyed experimenting with making lunch more than she'd expected. By the end of the first month, Nina noticed she had saved nearly $200 just by cutting back on these small, daily expenses.

Small expenses like daily coffees, impulse buys, and takeout lunches often feel harmless, but when compounded over time, they can become a significant drain on your finances. By trimming back or substituting more affordable options, you create room in your budget without feeling like you're making a big sacrifice. Nina's story highlights how even a modest change, like bringing lunch from home, can yield impressive savings when done consistently.

2. Eliminating Subscriptions and Memberships: "Need it, Use it, or Lose it"

After tackling daily expenses, Nina turned her attention to recurring costs. Like many people, she had subscriptions she'd forgotten about: a streaming service she rarely watched, a gym membership she hadn't used in months, and an app subscription she'd barely opened. While each subscription on its own didn't seem expensive, together, they added up to over $80 a month.

Nina adopted a new rule: "Need it, Use it, or Lose it." She canceled all subscriptions that didn't pass this simple test. To her surprise, she didn't even miss the services she'd dropped. The unused gym membership, in particular, had been a source of guilt, but letting it go felt like a relief. She replaced it with a set of weights and a yoga mat, creating a home workout routine that cost her nothing. Each canceled subscription became a win that empowered her to redirect those funds to a business savings account.

Many people fall into the same trap as Nina, thinking that "it's only $10 a month" or "I'll use it eventually." But subscriptions have a way of stacking up and eating away at your budget. Conducting a regular audit of recurring costs and getting rid of those that don't provide real value is a quick way to reclaim money without sacrificing anything meaningful.

3. Practicing "Mindful Spending" for Bigger Purchases

Next, Nina decided to address her spending on bigger-ticket items like clothes and tech gadgets. She enjoyed staying on-trend, and whenever she had a tough week or a big presentation, she rewarded herself with something new—a habit that had accumulated into a surprisingly large expense over time.

To change this, she adopted a "24-hour rule" for any non-essential purchase. If she saw something she liked, she waited 24 hours before buying it. During that time, she asked herself if the item aligned with her bigger goals. More often than not, she found the impulse passed, and she felt just as happy keeping that money in her account as she would have if she'd made the purchase.

The "24-hour rule" is a powerful technique for curbing impulse purchases. By pausing, you create a moment to check in with yourself, to weigh whether the purchase brings lasting value or if it's just a fleeting want. Over time, this habit can reshape your relationship with money, turning impulsive spending into intentional, growth-oriented decisions.

4. Redirecting Funds to Fuel Long-Term Growth

With newfound savings from her adjusted spending habits, Nina had a choice: She could let the money sit in her checking account, or she could redirect it toward something that supported her long-term goals. She opted to create two designated accounts: one for her "Business Fund" and another for a low-cost investment account that would grow over time. Each month, she set up an automatic transfer of the money she'd saved from her spending audit into these accounts.

Watching her "Business Fund" grow, Nina felt a renewed sense of purpose and motivation. She saw how each dollar she redirected was bringing her closer to her goal of starting her own business. The experience gave her a sense of control and empowerment, and she found herself less tempted to spend on things that didn't serve her vision. Her savings weren't just numbers on a screen; they were milestones toward a meaningful life goal.

5. Reaping the Rewards of Reallocation

Over time, Nina's new habits became second nature. She no longer saw them as sacrifices but as choices that allowed her to focus on what truly mattered. She treated herself occasionally but no longer relied on purchases for comfort or motivation. Instead, she began to associate fulfillment with the growth of her Business Fund and the investment account she'd set up. Each month, she felt proud of her progress and saw firsthand how small, smart decisions could create big changes in her life.

In just a year, Nina's reallocated savings had grown into a substantial amount—enough to cover several months of operating expenses for her future business. She felt confident and prepared to take the leap, knowing she'd built a financial foundation through mindful, purposeful spending.

Nina's journey is a testament to how a few thoughtful adjustments in spending can create a meaningful shift toward financial independence. By cutting unnecessary expenses, eliminating subscriptions, adopting mindful spending habits, and redirecting savings toward growth-oriented goals, she turned what once felt like small, inconsequential costs into significant contributions toward her future.

This approach to saving doesn't just lead to greater financial security; it also fosters a mindset of empowerment. Each dollar you save and redirect isn't just money—it's a step toward your dreams, your goals, and your personal vision of success. With intentional choices and the courage to look honestly at your spending, you can take control of your finances and create a life where every expense has purpose, every dollar has meaning, and every decision moves you closer to financial freedom.

# CHAPTER 5

## Investing Wisely

In the journey to financial freedom, saving is only half of the equation. The other half is knowing how to make your money work for you, growing it in ways that can outpace inflation and build lasting wealth. Investing isn't just for the wealthy or the experienced; it's a strategy available to anyone willing to learn and practice the right approach. This chapter will take you through the foundational aspects of investing, introducing the main types of investments—stocks, real estate, mutual funds, and more—and showing how each can play a part in your path toward your first million.

1. Understanding the Power of Investing

Consider the story of Jack, a young professional who was hesitant to start investing. He'd always thought the stock market was a risky place and preferred the safety of his savings account. But after several years, he noticed his savings weren't growing much, and inflation was quietly eroding his purchasing power. Jack knew he needed a different approach, but the idea of investing intimidated him. After all, he'd heard the cautionary tales: people who'd lost their life savings in bad stocks, real estate crashes, and failed ventures.

Jack decided to start small, beginning with a modest amount he could afford to lose if it didn't work out. He set out to learn the basics and discovered that investing wasn't about luck or guesswork but about strategy, knowledge, and calculated risk. Over time, he saw that even small, regular investments could grow significantly through the power of compound interest and market growth. Today, Jack's investments provide him with an additional income stream, setting him firmly on the path to financial independence.

Investing doesn't have to be a gamble, and it doesn't require perfect timing. By spreading investments across different assets and focusing on long-term growth, you can harness the power of investing with less risk and more confidence. Let's dive into some of the most common types of investments and explore how each one works, the potential risks, and the rewards.

2. Stocks: Ownership in Companies and the Power of Compounding

When you invest in stocks, you're buying a share of ownership in a company. As the company grows and becomes more profitable, the value of its stock typically increases, allowing you to sell it for a profit if you choose. Stocks are one of the most accessible and popular investment types, largely because they offer high growth potential.

Jenna is a perfect example of someone who built her wealth through consistent investment in stocks. As a teacher with a modest salary, she was initially cautious about investing. But after learning about the long-term growth potential of the stock market, Jenna began contributing small amounts each month to a brokerage account, buying shares in well-established companies. Over the years, her investments compounded, growing steadily even with market ups and downs. Today, she enjoys a portfolio that's worth significantly more than what she originally invested.

Stocks are often categorised by market capitalisation (large-cap, mid-cap, and small-cap) and by type (common and preferred). Each type has its own characteristics:

- Large-cap stocks are shares of well-established companies with a high market capitalisation, like Apple, Microsoft, and Google. These companies are generally considered safer investments but may offer lower returns compared to small-cap stocks.

- Mid-cap and small-cap stocks belong to medium and smaller companies that have higher growth potential but are often riskier.

- Common stocks give you voting rights and a claim on profits through dividends, while preferred stocks don't provide voting rights but often have fixed dividends, making them more stable.

Investing in stocks requires a long-term mindset and the ability to weather market fluctuations. Markets will go up and down, but over extended periods, they have historically provided an average return of about 7-10% annually. This means that with time and patience, even small investments in stocks can grow considerably through the power of compounding.

3. Real Estate: Building Wealth Through Property Ownership

Real estate has long been one of the most reliable ways to build wealth. When you invest in real estate, you're buying physical assets—land or property—that tend to appreciate over time and can generate passive income through rental payments.

Take Marissa, a pharmacist who initially had no experience in real estate. She saved diligently, then used her savings to purchase a small duplex. Marissa lived in one unit and rented out the other, allowing her to cover her mortgage payments with rental income. This "house-hacking" strategy enabled her to live affordably while building equity in her property. As the property's value appreciated, Marissa refinanced it, using the equity to buy a second rental property. Over the years, her real estate investments continued to grow, providing her with steady income and wealth she could pass down to her children.

Real estate investments can include various forms, each with its own pros and cons:

- Residential properties include single-family homes, condos, and multi-family buildings. They offer rental income and potential appreciation but require management and upkeep.

- Commercial properties (such as office spaces and retail buildings) often generate higher rental yields than residential properties, but they also come with higher risks and complexities, such as longer vacancies and economic sensitivity.

- REITs (Real Estate Investment Trusts) are companies that own, operate, or finance real estate that generates income. For those who want exposure to real estate without owning property, REITs provide an easy way to invest in real estate assets. They are traded on stock exchanges, making them as liquid as stocks.

Real estate investing requires upfront capital, but for those who are willing to learn the ropes, it can provide substantial returns. Additionally, real estate investments are often less volatile than stocks and provide an income stream, making them an attractive option for investors looking for stability and growth.

## 4. Mutual Funds and ETFs: Diversifying with Managed Portfolios

If you're looking for a way to invest in a variety of assets without having to pick individual stocks, mutual funds and exchange-traded funds (ETFs) might be the right choice. These funds pool money from multiple investors to invest in a diversified portfolio of assets, such as stocks, bonds, or other securities.

David, a young professional who didn't have the time or expertise to research individual stocks, chose to invest in mutual funds. By contributing regularly to an index fund, David was able to gain exposure to a wide range of companies with minimal risk. This diversified approach allowed him to benefit from the overall growth of the market, and he enjoyed peace of mind knowing his portfolio was spread across multiple assets.

- Mutual funds are managed by professionals who make investment decisions on behalf of investors. These funds can be actively managed (where a fund manager selects investments to try to outperform the market) or passively managed (such as index funds that mirror the performance of a particular market index).

- ETFs work similarly to mutual funds but are traded on stock exchanges, allowing you to buy and sell them like individual stocks. ETFs typically have lower fees than mutual funds and offer flexibility for those who want to invest in a specific sector or theme (e.g., technology, healthcare, or sustainable investing).

Both mutual funds and ETFs provide an easy way to diversify your investments without requiring in-depth market knowledge. They are often considered less risky than investing in individual stocks, as their performance reflects the combined performance of multiple assets. This diversification reduces the impact of any single asset's poor performance, making them a safer choice for new investors.

5. Bonds: Stability Through Fixed-Income Investments

Bonds are loans that investors make to corporations or governments in exchange for regular interest payments and the return of the principal amount at maturity. Bonds are generally less volatile than stocks, making them a popular choice for those seeking stability and predictable income.

Consider Helen, who was close to retirement and wanted to shift a portion of her portfolio to safer investments. She bought government bonds, which offered her regular interest payments and allowed her to preserve her capital with minimal risk. Bonds provided Helen with financial security, knowing she'd have a steady income even if the stock market experienced volatility.

Bonds come in various forms:

- Government bonds (such as U.S. Treasury bonds) are among the safest investments, as they're backed by the government. They offer lower returns but provide stability.

- Corporate bonds are issued by companies and offer higher returns than government bonds but come with higher risk, depending on the issuing company's financial health.

- Municipal bonds, issued by local governments, are often tax-exempt and appeal to investors looking to avoid taxes on investment income.

While bonds may not offer the high growth potential of stocks, they are a valuable component in a diversified portfolio, especially as you approach financial milestones or prioritise income stability.

## 6. Alternative Investments: Exploring Gold, Cryptocurrencies, and Commodities

For those interested in diversification beyond traditional assets, alternative investments offer unique opportunities. These investments can include assets like gold, cryptocurrencies, and commodities, each providing different levels of risk and growth potential.

Aaron, a tech-savvy investor, was particularly drawn to cryptocurrencies. He'd always been fascinated by emerging technology, and while he knew that digital assets were volatile, he decided to allocate a small portion of his portfolio to Bitcoin and Ethereum. He balanced these high-risk assets with more stable investments, like stocks and bonds, so that his portfolio could withstand market swings.

While alternative investments aren't for everyone, they can be an exciting way to diversify if approached carefully:

- Gold is often viewed as a hedge against inflation and market instability. It doesn't provide the growth of stocks, but it can be a safe-haven asset during economic uncertainty.

- Cryptocurrencies like Bitcoin and Ethereum have gained popularity in recent years due to their high growth potential, though they are highly volatile and should only constitute a small portion of a balanced portfolio.

- Commodities (like oil, agricultural products, and metals) offer exposure to different sectors of the economy and are often uncorrelated with the stock market, making them useful for diversification.

Alternative investments should be approached with caution and a clear understanding of the risks involved. They can add diversity to a portfolio but shouldn't replace more reliable assets.

Each type of investment serves a different purpose and comes with its own risks and rewards. For Max, a young entrepreneur with a taste for adventure, stocks and cryptocurrencies were appealing. For Linda, who was nearing retirement, bonds and REITs provided the stability she valued. And for James, a middle-aged professional building a diverse portfolio, mutual funds and real estate were the core of his long-term strategy.

The key to investing wisely is to understand your financial goals, risk tolerance, and timeline. A balanced portfolio that combines various asset types allows you to capitalise on growth while minimising risk. You don't need a large sum to start investing; what's more important is consistency and a willingness to learn. With each investment, you're taking a step closer to financial independence, building wealth that can provide security and freedom for the years to come.

Investing isn't just about growing wealth; it's about taking control of your financial future, making informed choices, and letting your money work for you. With patience and discipline, your investments will become a powerful ally in achieving your first million and beyond.

Risk management is one of the most critical aspects of investing and is essential to protecting your wealth as you grow it. While investing is one of the best ways to build financial security and achieve long-term goals, it comes with inherent risks. Understanding how much to invest and where to allocate your funds is central to managing these risks effectively. This means knowing how much of your capital you're comfortable putting on the line, balancing higher-risk assets with more stable investments, and adopting strategies that fit your unique risk tolerance and financial objectives.

To illustrate the importance of risk management, consider Chris, a 35-year-old engineer who was determined to grow his savings through investing. Inspired by stories of people who had made quick fortunes in high-flying tech stocks, Chris put almost all his savings into a handful of trending tech companies. For a while, the strategy seemed to work—his portfolio grew quickly, and he felt like a savvy investor. But then the market took a downturn, and his stocks, which were highly volatile, dropped in value almost overnight. Without a risk management plan in place, Chris found himself in a tight financial spot, his portfolio having lost nearly half its value.

After this experience, Chris decided to reassess his approach to investing and adopted a diversified, risk-managed strategy instead. Here's how he turned things around, balancing his portfolio to protect his capital while still achieving growth.

1. Determining Your Risk Tolerance: How Much Can You Afford to Lose?

The first step in risk management is determining your personal risk tolerance—essentially, how much risk you're comfortable taking on. Risk tolerance depends on various factors, including your financial goals, timeline, and personality. If you're naturally risk-averse, putting too much of your portfolio in high-volatility assets like individual stocks or cryptocurrencies might cause you undue stress. On the other hand, if you're young with a long investment horizon, you might be willing to take on more risk to achieve higher returns.

Risk tolerance also depends on your current financial situation. Consider Sarah, a single mom with two children, who works in a stable but modest job. She wants to build wealth for her children's future but is conscious of her financial responsibilities. For Sarah, a low-risk, conservative approach focused on stable investments like bonds and dividend-paying stocks aligns better with her goals and her financial capacity.

A helpful way to determine your risk tolerance is to think about how you would feel in different market conditions. Would you be able to remain calm and patient if your portfolio dropped by 20% in a market downturn? If not, it might make sense to focus on a more conservative asset mix that provides a balance of growth and stability.

## 2. Allocating Funds Across Different Asset Classes: Diversifying Your Portfolio

Once you've established your risk tolerance, the next step is deciding where to invest. The goal is to spread your investments across different types of assets to reduce the impact of a downturn in any single area. This is the principle of diversification, and it's one of the most effective ways to manage risk.

Let's look at Jasmine, a small business owner who started investing in her late twenties. Jasmine wanted to maximise her returns, but after doing her research, she realised that putting all her money into one asset class—such as stocks—would make her portfolio too volatile. Instead, she decided to diversify by allocating 60% of her portfolio to stocks (for growth), 20% to bonds (for stability and income), 10% to real estate (for long-term appreciation), and 10% to cash or cash-equivalents (for liquidity).

By diversifying her portfolio, Jasmine protected herself from major losses. If the stock market took a hit, her bonds and real estate investments would help cushion the blow. Diversifying across multiple asset classes allows investors like Jasmine to balance growth with security, making it easier to weather market fluctuations while still achieving returns.

3. Setting Investment Limits: How Much to Allocate to Each Investment

Once you've decided on the types of assets you want to invest in, the next step is setting specific limits for each investment. Allocating too much to a single asset—say, putting 80% of your portfolio into one company's stock—can lead to significant losses if that asset underperforms. Even within asset classes, it's wise to avoid over-committing to any one investment.

Daniel, a tech enthusiast, was drawn to the rapid growth of technology stocks. At first, he invested almost exclusively in the tech sector, as it was where he felt most comfortable. But after consulting with a financial advisor, he realized that he had "concentration risk"—the risk associated with investing heavily in a single sector. Daniel then decided to limit his exposure to tech stocks to 40% of his portfolio, with the remainder spread across healthcare, financials, and consumer goods. By setting these limits, Daniel was able to stay invested in his preferred sector while managing his overall risk.

4. Rebalancing: Adjusting Your Portfolio to Stay Aligned with Your Goals

As markets fluctuate, your portfolio's asset allocation can drift from its original plan. Rebalancing is the process of realigning your investments to maintain your desired asset allocation. This helps you avoid "drift" where certain investments become over-weighted, which can increase risk.

For example, Alex, a 40-year-old investor with a balanced portfolio of 60% stocks and 40% bonds, experienced significant growth in his stock holdings over a few years. This growth shifted his portfolio to 75% stocks and 25% bonds, increasing his exposure to market volatility. By rebalancing—selling some stocks and buying more bonds—Alex was able to bring his portfolio back to its original allocation, reducing risk and ensuring he was positioned for stable growth.

Rebalancing can be done on a regular basis, such as once a year, or whenever there is a significant shift in your portfolio's asset allocation. This approach keeps you aligned with your risk tolerance and long-term goals, helping you navigate changes in the market without overexposing yourself.

5. Emergency Funds and Liquidity: Preparing for the Unexpected

One often-overlooked aspect of risk management is maintaining liquidity—having cash or easily accessible funds in case of emergencies. While the goal of investing is to grow wealth, life can be unpredictable, and it's essential to have liquid assets on hand for unexpected expenses.

Michelle, a young professional with a budding investment portfolio, learned the importance of liquidity when her car broke down unexpectedly. Because she had set aside an emergency fund in a high-yield savings account, she was able to cover the repair costs without having to dip into her investments. This allowed her to keep her long-term investments intact, avoiding any potential losses from selling assets in a down market.

Having a cash cushion means you won't have to liquidate investments prematurely to cover unexpected costs. Most experts recommend setting aside at least three to six months' worth of living expenses in an emergency fund. This provides peace of mind and protects your investments, allowing them to grow uninterrupted.

6. Understanding Risk-Return Trade-offs: Balancing Safety with Growth Potential

Every investment comes with a risk-return trade-off, which means that higher potential returns usually come with higher risks. Balancing this trade-off is key to building a portfolio that aligns with your goals.

Consider Evan, an investor who wanted high returns to build wealth quickly. Initially, he was drawn to high-risk assets like emerging tech stocks and small-cap companies, which promised rapid growth. However, after several volatile years, Evan realised that his portfolio's swings were too stressful and inconsistent with his long-term goals. He re-evaluated his approach, shifting 30% of his funds to safer, income-generating assets like bonds and dividend-paying stocks. This adjustment allowed Evan to capture some growth potential while also maintaining stability.

By understanding the risk-return trade-off, investors can choose assets that reflect their financial goals. Younger investors with longer time horizons may lean more toward growth assets like stocks, while those closer to retirement may prioritise stability and income generation.

7. The Role of Education and Due Diligence: Knowing Where You're Investing

One of the best ways to manage risk is through education and thorough research. Understanding the assets you're investing in can help you make better decisions, recognise red flags, and avoid costly mistakes.

Linda, a novice investor, was initially drawn to high-yield investment options she'd seen advertised online, including some that promised guaranteed returns. Instead of diving in, she took the time to learn about these offers, discovering that many were actually scams or high-risk speculative investments. By educating herself, Linda was able to avoid falling victim to potential fraud and redirected her funds into safer, diversified investments.

Conducting due diligence—researching each asset, understanding its risks, and being aware of market trends—empowers you to make informed choices. Investing blindly or following trends without understanding them can lead to losses, so taking the time to learn is an essential part of managing risk.

Risk management is the foundation of a successful investment strategy. Knowing how much to invest, where to invest, and setting clear limits and guidelines can safeguard your wealth while allowing it to grow. Through real-world examples like those of Chris, Jasmine, Daniel, and others, we've seen how a balanced approach to risk—one that involves diversification, emergency planning, rebalancing, and ongoing education—can help you achieve steady growth without exposing yourself to unnecessary risk.

Remember, investing isn't about avoiding risk altogether; it's about managing it wisely. A well-diversified portfolio, combined with a disciplined approach to rebalancing and a firm understanding of your goals and risk tolerance, will put you on a steady path toward financial freedom. By taking control of the risks associated with investing, you're not just protecting your wealth—you're building the confidence and resilience needed to reach your first million and beyond.

Compounding is often called the "eighth wonder of the world" for a reason. It's a financial principle so simple yet so powerful that, when used correctly, it can create exponential growth in your wealth over time. To truly appreciate the magic of compounding, imagine it as a snowball rolling down a hill, gathering snow as it goes. Each rotation builds on the last, creating a momentum that turns a small ball into a massive one by the time it reaches the bottom. This is how compounding works with your money: the more it grows, the faster it gathers momentum, ultimately transforming even small investments into significant wealth over time.

The Power of Time: A Story of Two Friends

To see compounding in action, let's look at the story of two friends, Emma and Laura. Both started working in their twenties, and both wanted to start saving for retirement. Emma, eager to get a head start, began putting $200 a month into an investment account that earned an average of 8% interest per year. Laura, on the other hand, felt she had more time and decided to wait until she was thirty-five to start investing the same amount each month.

By the time they both reached sixty-five, Emma's account had grown to nearly $700,000, while Laura's account, despite investing the same amount monthly, had only grown to around $250,000. How did this happen? Compounding.

Emma's head start allowed her investment returns to compound over more years, making her wealth grow exponentially. Every year, her interest earned interest, and her balance grew faster. Laura invested the same amount but didn't give her money as much time to compound. As a result, she missed out on the incredible growth that could have come from letting her money sit and multiply.

The lesson here is simple: the earlier you start, the more time you give your money to grow, and the more powerful compounding becomes.

## Reinvestment: Letting Your Returns Work for You

One of the core elements of compounding is reinvestment. When you earn money on an investment, reinvesting it—rather than taking it out—allows that money to start generating returns of its own. Think of compounding as a chain reaction, where every gain you make becomes the foundation for future growth.

Take Jack, for example. Jack invested in a mutual fund that offered dividend reinvestment, meaning any profits he made were automatically reinvested into the fund. By not touching the dividends, Jack allowed them to keep growing. The initial investment, along with his reinvested dividends, created a "snowball effect" that turned his modest contributions into a robust retirement fund. Jack didn't have to do any extra work; the reinvestment kept building on itself, steadily increasing his wealth.

Compounding doesn't necessarily require large sums; even small amounts, when reinvested consistently, can result in considerable wealth over time. Reinvestment is one of the most critical aspects of compounding because it uses your returns to make even more returns.

The Rule of 72: Doubling Your Money

One of the most exciting aspects of compounding is how quickly it can double your money when given the right conditions. Financial experts often talk about the Rule of 72, which is a simple formula to estimate how long it will take for an investment to double given a fixed annual rate of return. By dividing 72 by the expected rate of return, you get the approximate number of years it will take for your money to double.

Let's return to Emma for a moment. With an 8% rate of return, she could expect her money to double every nine years ($72 \div 8 = 9$). This means that, without adding any new funds, her initial investment would multiply repeatedly over her lifetime. In fact, each doubling brings with it more and more growth, so that later "doublings" yield much larger amounts than the earlier ones.

Understanding the Rule of 72 can be a powerful motivator for staying invested and patient. Every year that passes brings you closer to the next "doubling" milestone, a reminder that time is your ally in compounding.

Small Investments, Big Returns: The Coffee Experiment

Sometimes, people feel they don't have enough money to invest to make a difference. But compounding shows that even small contributions can lead to big returns when given enough time. To illustrate this, financial experts often use the example of daily coffee habits.

Imagine Michael, a young professional who buys a $4 coffee every day. That's roughly $120 per month. If Michael decided to skip his daily coffee and instead invested that money in an account earning a 7% annual return, he'd have over $100,000 in 20 years. It might not seem like much on a day-to-day basis, but those small amounts add up due to compounding.

This example demonstrates that even minor lifestyle adjustments can have a huge impact over time. Compounding allows small sacrifices in the present to turn into major financial gains in the future. By redirecting even modest amounts into investments, you set up a powerful compounding machine that grows steadily over time.

The Patience Factor: Staying Invested Through Ups and Downs

One of the most critical aspects of compounding is the ability to stay invested, especially when markets are volatile. Compounding works best when left undisturbed; every time you pull money out of an investment, you interrupt the growth process.

Consider Alex, who was initially enthusiastic about his investments. He started with a well-balanced portfolio, but during a market downturn, he got nervous and decided to pull out his funds to "wait until things looked better." By doing so, he missed out on the market recovery that followed, essentially locking in his losses and preventing his investments from compounding during the rebound.

Alex's experience is a reminder that compounding requires patience and a long-term perspective. While the market can have ups and downs, staying invested allows you to capture the long-term growth that compounding can offer. By riding out the low points, you keep your investments growing, which is where the true power of compounding shines.

Creating a Legacy Through Compounding

One of the most profound impacts of compounding is its ability to create wealth that can be passed down through generations. By staying invested and allowing wealth to compound over time, you're not just building a financial future for yourself—you're creating a legacy.

Take the story of Marion, who started a small investment portfolio in her twenties and watched it grow over decades. By the time she reached retirement, Marion had amassed significant wealth, far more than she ever thought possible. Instead of using it all for herself, she decided to pass down a portion of her investments to her children and grandchildren. Thanks to the power of compounding, this money will continue to grow, benefiting her family for generations to come.

Compounding transforms wealth-building into something beyond personal gain; it's a way to create long-lasting financial security for loved ones. With enough time, even a modest initial investment can grow into something substantial, leaving a legacy that continues to build wealth long after you're gone.

Compounding is the quiet force behind some of the world's greatest fortunes. It doesn't require constant management or an extensive financial background; it simply requires time, patience, and consistency. The earlier you start, the more opportunities you create for your wealth to multiply, growing from small beginnings into significant financial security.

Whether you're investing in stocks, real estate, or a high-interest savings account, the principle of compounding applies. By reinvesting your returns and staying the course, you allow your money to work for you, building momentum over time. Just like Emma, Jack, and Marion, you, too, can harness the power of compounding to create a future that's financially secure, resilient, and filled with possibilities. The journey might start small, but compounding ensures that each step forward makes the next one even stronger, bringing you closer to your first million and beyond.

# CHAPTER 6

## Building and Scaling a Business

In Building and Scaling a Business, we dive into the power of entrepreneurship as a path to financial freedom and building your first million. Many self-made millionaires didn't rely solely on traditional jobs or single income streams. Instead, they ventured into the world of business, creating something scalable and enduring. In this chapter, we'll break down the fundamentals of entrepreneurship and explore business ideas that can grow alongside you. Whether it's a side hustle you can scale or a startup with potential to disrupt an industry, the entrepreneurial journey is one of the most powerful ways to amass wealth and create a life of freedom.

## The Entrepreneurial Mindset: Embracing Opportunity and Resilience

Before diving into specific business ideas or models, we must start with the mindset that fuels successful entrepreneurship. Building a business isn't just about profits; it's about problem-solving, resilience, and adaptability. Consider Tommy, a college graduate who felt trapped in a nine-to-five job that didn't inspire him. He started looking for gaps in the market where he could add value, initially just for extra income. His focus was on identifying problems people had and finding creative ways to solve them.

Tommy's story is common among entrepreneurs. He realised that in every market, there's always room for improvement, for something faster, simpler, or more convenient. His determination to address real-world needs became his foundation. While he faced numerous setbacks—product returns, marketing challenges, and funding shortfalls—his resilience helped him navigate these obstacles. This entrepreneurial mindset, one that embraces opportunity and learns from setbacks, is foundational for building any successful business.

Identifying Scalable Business Ideas: Solving Problems with Long-Term Potential

When it comes to choosing the right business to build, scalability is key. Many people start businesses that only succeed on a small scale because they're based on trading time for money without an easy path to growth. Scalable businesses, on the other hand, can grow with limited increases in costs, allowing you to reach more people without a proportional increase in expenses.

Take Sarah, a skilled graphic designer who began her career freelancing. She soon realised that no matter how many clients she took on, she could only work so many hours. To scale, she started designing pre-made templates and branding kits she could sell to many customers online. By shifting her focus from one-on-one services to products that were reusable and scalable, Sarah tapped into a passive income stream that allowed her to multiply her earnings without increasing her workload. Today, she sells thousands of templates a month, reaching customers worldwide and far exceeding what she could have earned as a freelancer.

This example highlights a key lesson: when thinking about business ideas, consider ways to create products, platforms, or services that can serve multiple customers simultaneously.

The Basics of Launching Your Business: From Idea to Execution

Once you've identified a scalable business idea, the next step is to bring it to life. Turning an idea into a profitable business requires focus on three main areas: product development, market validation, and branding.

1. Product Development: Building a product or service that people will buy is the first step. This could be anything from a physical product to an online

course, a mobile app, or even a subscription service. The key is to create something valuable that addresses a specific pain point or enhances someone's life in a meaningful way.

2. Market Validation: Before investing too much time or money, validate your idea with real people. Consider Jackie, who had an idea for a pet subscription box filled with toys and treats. Instead of jumping straight into production, she created a simple website describing the service and ran a few Facebook ads to test interest. The response was overwhelming, giving Jackie the confidence to proceed. Market validation allows you to test ideas without a huge initial investment and learn what your audience really wants.

3. Branding: Branding goes beyond logos and color schemes; it's about the experience and trust you build with your customers. A strong brand tells a story, connects emotionally with customers, and helps you stand out in a crowded market. For instance, Raj, a young entrepreneur in the fitness industry, launched a high-quality line of fitness apparel that resonated with people not just because of the products but because his brand focused on self-empowerment and inclusivity. His customers felt like they were part of a larger community, which kept them coming back and spreading the word.

These early stages can be some of the most challenging and exciting parts of entrepreneurship. Each step requires attention, persistence, and the willingness to learn quickly from feedback and mistakes.

Creating Leverage: Building Systems and Delegating Tasks

Building a business that scales involves more than just great products or services; it's about creating systems and structures that allow your business to operate efficiently, even when you're not directly involved. The difference between a self-employed business owner and a scalable entrepreneur often comes down to the ability to leverage other people, systems, and technology.

Anita, for example, started her e-commerce business from her garage, fulfilling every order herself and handling every detail from customer service to packaging. But as her business grew, she quickly realised she couldn't do it all alone. By hiring a small team and using fulfillment software, she was able to automate many parts of her business. This allowed her to step back from day-to-day operations and focus on growing her company further.

The lesson here is that if you want to scale, you need to think beyond yourself. This means creating processes, delegating tasks, and leveraging technology so that your business can grow independently of your own time and energy.

Funding Your Venture: Understanding Financing Options

Financing is often one of the biggest challenges for new entrepreneurs, especially if they're working with limited capital. While some businesses can be started on a shoestring budget, others may require significant upfront investment. Understanding the types of funding available can help you choose the best option for your business.

1. Self-Funding: Many entrepreneurs start by self-funding their ventures, using personal savings or income from a current job to get their business off the ground. This approach allows you to maintain full control of your company but can be risky if it strains your personal finances.

2. Angel Investors and Venture Capital: For businesses with high growth potential, angel investors or venture capital (VC) funding can provide the capital needed to scale quickly. In exchange for an equity stake, these investors offer large sums of money to help grow the business, although this often means sharing decision-making power.

3. Crowdfunding: Crowdfunding has become a popular way to fund projects by raising small amounts of money from a large number of people. Platforms like Kickstarter and Indiegogo allow entrepreneurs to pitch their ideas to a wide audience and gain initial funding without giving up equity.

4. Small Business Loans and Grants: Traditional bank loans or government grants can provide necessary funding with fixed terms. This option works well for entrepreneurs who want to retain full ownership but may require strong credit or a solid business plan to secure the loan.

Miguel, a restaurant owner, used a combination of self-funding and a small business loan to open his first location. By minimizing expenses and gradually building his customer base, he was able to scale up over time, eventually opening multiple locations. By understanding financing options and balancing risk with opportunity, Miguel turned a single restaurant into a regional franchise.

## Marketing and Customer Acquisition: Reaching and Retaining Your Audience

No matter how good your product or service is, a business cannot thrive without customers. Effective marketing and customer acquisition strategies are essential for scaling a business and ensuring long-term success.

Lily, a wellness coach, knew she had valuable services to offer, but she struggled to get her message out. She invested in online marketing, specifically social media and email campaigns, to build awareness. Through regular content that provided value—like wellness tips, testimonials, and success stories—she slowly built a loyal audience. Eventually, her following became her customer base, allowing her to convert online engagements into paying clients.

Marketing doesn't have to be complicated, but it does require consistency. Building an email list, connecting through social media, and running ads can help drive traffic and build brand recognition. Once you have customers, focus on retaining them by providing exceptional service, listening to their feedback, and creating a brand experience they'll want to return to.

Scaling Strategically: Expanding with Purpose

Scaling a business doesn't always mean rapid growth. Strategic scaling is about expanding sustainably, ensuring that each step forward builds on a solid foundation. Once your business is established, there are several ways to scale:

1. Expanding Product Lines or Services: You can scale by adding complementary products or services that meet additional customer needs. For example, if you run an online store selling skincare products, adding a line of hair care or beauty accessories can increase your customer's value per purchase.

2. Entering New Markets: Consider expanding geographically or targeting new demographics. This could mean moving from a local to a national market or adapting your offerings to appeal to a different age group.

3. Forming Partnerships: Partnerships with other businesses can help you scale by sharing resources, reaching more customers, and creating joint marketing initiatives. Collaborations can boost brand visibility and provide mutual benefits without huge investments.

4. Franchising or Licensing: For some businesses, franchising or licensing is a way to scale rapidly. This model allows other people to operate under your brand, giving you access to new markets without the need for hands-on management of each new location.

Ben, who founded a small fitness studio, initially expanded by offering additional services like personal training and nutrition counseling. Once demand grew, he franchised his studio model, allowing others to open studios in new cities. This approach allowed him to scale while maintaining quality and brand consistency, and his business became a multi-million-dollar operation.

Building a Legacy: Entrepreneurship as a Path to Wealth and Freedom

Starting and scaling a business is not only a path to achieving your first million but also a journey to freedom and legacy. Entrepreneurship allows you to create something of value, an asset that can continue to grow and generate wealth even when you step away. This journey is not for the faint-hearted, as it requires dedication, resilience, and a willingness to learn from failures. But for those who embrace it, the rewards go far beyond financial gains.

By building a business, you're creating an impact in the world, solving real problems, and potentially leaving something lasting for future generations. For many, entrepreneurship is the ultimate expression of financial freedom, a path where they call the shots, build something meaningful, and ultimately create wealth on their own terms.

Identifying and Meeting Market Needs

In the world of entrepreneurship, identifying and meeting market needs is the cornerstone of success.

Building a business isn't just about creating a product or service; it's about ensuring that what you offer genuinely solves a problem or satisfies a desire that people care about. Many successful entrepreneurs have mastered the art of tuning into what the market truly needs, enabling them to create impactful solutions that drive lasting success. In this chapter, we'll explore how to understand market needs deeply, identify opportunities, and deliver value with purpose and precision.

## The Entrepreneur's Golden Rule: Find the Gap

Imagine you're an aspiring entrepreneur, watching successful companies that seem to have hit the mark perfectly with their products. You might ask yourself, How did they know this was what people wanted? The answer, more often than not, lies in their ability to find a gap in the market—a need that hasn't yet been addressed or isn't being served well.

Consider Emily, a young woman who was frustrated with the limited options for sustainable household products. She wanted to find cleaning supplies that were eco-friendly, affordable, and genuinely effective, but every brand she encountered seemed to fall short in one of these areas. Emily saw this gap as an opportunity: she decided to create her own line of sustainable products that met these criteria. By focusing on an underserved need, Emily tapped into a growing demand for eco-friendly products and built a business with a loyal customer base who shared her values.

Emily's story highlights the importance of finding gaps in existing markets. Spotting these opportunities requires a keen eye, an open mind, and the willingness to ask, What's missing? Often, your own frustrations and observations can be a powerful starting point. By recognizing where current offerings fall short, you set yourself up to develop a unique and valuable solution.

Researching Market Needs: The Power of Listening

Understanding what the market needs begins with one of the simplest yet most powerful tools in an entrepreneur's toolkit: listening. Successful businesses are built by entrepreneurs who listen to customers, observe their behaviors, and tune into their preferences. In an era where consumer demands are constantly evolving, it's critical to stay connected to your audience and pay attention to what they're saying—directly and indirectly.

Jason, a small business owner in the fitness industry, decided to create a new line of workout equipment after repeatedly hearing complaints from his clients. They loved working out at home but found that most home gym equipment was bulky and difficult to store. Jason spent months listening to feedback and researching home fitness trends. He found that more people were seeking compact, versatile equipment that allowed them to maintain an active lifestyle without dedicating an entire room to fitness gear.

By listening attentively to his clients' frustrations, Jason developed a line of space-saving, multifunctional equipment that quickly became popular. He didn't invent something entirely new; instead, he improved upon what was already available, meeting the specific needs of his market. Listening, as Jason demonstrated, can be the key to uncovering insights that guide you toward a viable product.

Listening can take many forms—casual conversations, online forums, social media comments, or even customer reviews of competitors. Each provides a window into what potential customers value, what they dislike, and what solutions they're searching for.

Using Data and Trends to Identify Market Needs

Another powerful tool in identifying market needs is data. In today's digital world, data is everywhere, offering insights that would have been difficult to access just a few years ago. Entrepreneurs can now analyze trends, study consumer behavior, and understand preferences by tapping into available data sources.

Sara, a recent college graduate, wanted to launch a clothing line but wasn't sure what niche would set her apart in the crowded fashion industry. She turned to trend analysis, using data from Google Trends, Instagram, and fashion forecasting platforms to track what was gaining popularity. She noticed a significant rise in demand for gender-neutral clothing and decided to focus her brand on offering minimalist, versatile pieces that appealed to a broad demographic.

Her data-driven approach helped her target a growing niche, positioning her brand as a frontrunner in gender-neutral fashion. Using data allowed Sara to make an informed decision rather than relying solely on instinct. This strategy helped her hit the ground running with a clear focus on what her target audience wanted.

Data can provide powerful insights if you know where to look. Some of the most accessible sources of market data include:

- Google Trends: Tracks the popularity of search queries over time, highlighting rising topics and interests.
- Social Media Analytics: Platforms like Instagram, Twitter, and Facebook allow you to monitor

engagement, spot trends, and understand what resonates with audiences.

- Industry Reports: Many industries produce reports on consumer behavior, emerging trends, and market needs that can provide valuable insights.

By analyzing data, you're not just guessing what the market might need—you're backing your ideas with evidence that reflects real consumer interests.

Empathy and Observation: Stepping into Your Customers' Shoes

One of the most profound ways to identify market needs is through empathy and observation. This approach requires you to step into the shoes of your potential customers, seeing the world from their perspective. Sometimes, market needs aren't obvious until you experience them firsthand or observe them closely.

Consider the case of Rajesh, a father who struggled to find healthy, convenient snacks for his children. He noticed that most snacks marketed to kids were either highly processed or didn't appeal to their taste buds. As a parent, he felt the frustration of choosing between health and convenience, and he realized that other parents likely shared his struggle. Rajesh decided to develop a line of healthy, kid-friendly snacks that balanced nutrition with taste, creating a product that met the needs of health-conscious parents.

Rajesh's journey demonstrates the power of empathy. By observing his own challenges and understanding the concerns of other parents, he was able to identify a clear market need. Empathy often reveals unmet needs that might not be obvious through data alone, making it an invaluable tool in the entrepreneurial process.

Testing and Validating Your Idea: Making Sure the Market Wants It

Once you've identified a potential need, the next step is to test and validate your idea. Testing allows you to gauge market interest before investing significant time or resources, helping you avoid the trap of launching a product that no one wants.

Linda, an aspiring entrepreneur, had an idea for a subscription box service that offered unique self-care items each month. Before committing fully, she decided to test her concept with a small group of potential customers. She created a simple website, ran a few social media ads, and offered a discount for early subscribers. The positive response confirmed her idea's viability, giving her the confidence to proceed.

Testing doesn't have to be complicated. Simple strategies like creating a landing page, running pre-orders, or offering early-bird discounts can reveal whether there's genuine interest in your product. If people are willing to pay, you have solid evidence that you're on the right track.

Refining Your Offering: Adapting to Feedback and Evolving Market Needs

Market needs are rarely static—they change over time, influenced by trends, technology, and consumer expectations. Successful entrepreneurs understand the importance of staying flexible and open to feedback, refining their offerings to keep pace with evolving market demands.

Mark, a tech entrepreneur, developed a project management app for small businesses. Initially, his app included a few basic features, but as he listened to user feedback, he learned that his customers wanted additional tools for team collaboration. Rather than sticking rigidly to his original concept, Mark adapted, incorporating new features based on what his users wanted. This adaptability helped him build a loyal customer base and grow his app into a leading tool for small business owners.

Feedback is invaluable in the journey of meeting market needs. Regularly asking for customer input and staying responsive to requests allows you to refine your product and build a stronger connection with your audience. Entrepreneurs who prioritize customer feedback are better positioned to adapt and grow in competitive markets.

Addressing Unmet Needs and Creating Unique Value Propositions

Identifying market needs isn't just about meeting existing demands; it's also about discovering unmet needs that others haven't yet addressed. Unmet needs represent opportunities to create unique value propositions—solutions that are different from anything else on the market.

Chloe, a former athlete, noticed that many fitness apps focused heavily on high-intensity workouts, but few catered to individuals recovering from injuries or dealing with chronic pain. Recognizing this gap, she developed an app tailored to people with special fitness needs, offering gentle workouts and guidance on injury prevention. By addressing an underserved segment, Chloe created a product that offered unique value and stood out in the crowded fitness app market.

A unique value proposition differentiates your product from competitors, giving customers a compelling reason to choose you. By identifying and meeting unmet needs, you're not just competing in the market—you're carving out a distinct place within it.

Balancing Innovation and Practicality: Knowing When to Push Boundaries

Innovation can be a powerful driver of success, but it's essential to balance creativity with practicality. Not every bold idea will align with market needs, and some innovations may require education or gradual adoption. Entrepreneurs must consider whether their market is ready for what they're offering and whether their idea is feasible.

Leo, a tech innovator, developed a cutting-edge home automation system with complex features. However, he discovered that his target customers found it overwhelming and preferred simpler solutions. Instead of abandoning his concept, Leo adapted by simplifying his product, focusing on core features that addressed the most common needs. This pragmatic approach allowed him to introduce innovation in a way that resonated with his audience.

The balance between innovation and practicality is key. Pushing boundaries is valuable, but aligning your offering with customer expectations and readiness ensures that your innovations are embraced, not rejected.

## Fostering a Culture of Curiosity and Adaptability

The most successful entrepreneurs view the journey of meeting market needs as an ongoing process. They foster a culture of curiosity, continually asking questions and seeking ways to improve. This mindset helps them stay ahead of trends, adapt to changes, and remain relevant.

Sophia, the founder of a skincare brand, attributes her success to her relentless curiosity. She regularly surveys her customers, attends industry conferences, and experiments with new ingredients. Her willingness to explore, learn, and adapt keeps her brand fresh and responsive to market shifts.

Curiosity and adaptability are invaluable traits in today's fast-paced business world. By staying open to new information and continuously seeking to understand market needs, entrepreneurs can evolve their offerings and sustain success over time.

In summary, meeting market needs is an art and a science. It requires listening, researching, empathizing, testing, and adapting. By approaching this process with an open mind and a focus on delivering genuine value, you can create a business that resonates deeply with its audience and stands the test of time. Identifying and meeting market needs isn't just about making money—it's about creating something meaningful, fulfilling unmet desires, and ultimately contributing to a better world.

Strategies for Scaling a Small Business for Significant Profit

Scaling a business is both an art and a science. For many small business owners, the idea of growing their venture into a larger, more profitable enterprise can feel daunting. But the key to significant growth often lies in implementing thoughtful, strategic actions designed to expand your reach, increase revenue, and streamline operations. This chapter will dive deep into the strategies that transform a small business into a profitable powerhouse, exploring real-world examples and providing actionable insights to help entrepreneurs scale effectively.

The Foundation of Scaling: Getting the Basics Right

When it comes to scaling, there's no shortcut. Before you can grow, you need a solid foundation. Scaling a business without first ensuring stability and consistency is like building a skyscraper on shaky ground. To ensure you're ready for expansion, take the time to evaluate your core operations, your value proposition, and the quality of your offerings.

Consider Mia, who launched a small organic skincare line out of her home. Her business began modestly, selling products at local markets and through an online store. After gaining traction, Mia started receiving wholesale inquiries from larger retailers. But before she could pursue these opportunities, she realized she needed to address a few key issues: refining her manufacturing process, standardizing product quality, and building a reliable supply chain. Mia knew that without these pieces in place, she risked not being able to fulfill larger orders or, worse, damaging her brand reputation.

By taking the time to strengthen her operations, Mia set herself up for sustainable growth. She created documented processes, built relationships with trustworthy suppliers, and invested in quality control. This foundation allowed her to scale with confidence, ultimately securing partnerships with national retailers and significantly increasing her profits. Her experience illustrates the importance of stabilizing your business before focusing on expansion.

## Developing a Scalable Business Model

One of the critical factors in scaling is having a business model that can grow without excessive complications. This often means building processes that don't rely solely on you, the owner, to run smoothly. A scalable model allows you to handle higher demand without constantly needing to add resources, hire additional staff, or micromanage operations.

Darren, a consultant specializing in financial planning for small businesses, initially worked with clients one-on-one. He quickly realized that this model, while effective, wasn't scalable. He could only serve so many clients per week, and increasing his client load meant sacrificing his personal time and energy. Darren decided to explore options that would allow him to reach more people without working longer hours.

He created an online course and an e-book that distilled his most valuable insights into easily accessible content. Not only did this allow him to reach a wider audience, but it also created passive income streams that could continue generating revenue without his direct involvement. Darren's transition to a scalable model enabled him to serve thousands of clients instead of dozens, significantly increasing his income while reducing his time spent on direct client work.

A scalable business model often includes products or services that can be easily replicated or delivered to larger audiences. Examples include digital products, online courses, subscription-based models, or services that utilize automation. By developing a scalable model, you open the door to exponential growth.

Leveraging Technology for Efficiency

In today's digital world, technology is one of the most powerful tools for scaling. Automation, customer relationship management (CRM) software, and analytics tools can all help you streamline operations and handle growth more effectively. Technology can save you time, reduce costs, and enable you to deliver a consistent experience as your business grows.

Jasmine, a restaurant owner, was struggling to keep up with customer orders, especially during busy lunch hours. She noticed that customers were getting frustrated with wait times, which hurt her business's reputation and affected repeat visits. To address this, Jasmine implemented an online ordering system that allowed customers to place orders from their phones and pick them up without waiting in line.

The system not only improved customer satisfaction but also allowed Jasmine to serve more customers without adding additional staff. This simple technological upgrade made her business more efficient and prepared her for future growth. Jasmine's experience highlights how technology can be a game-changer in scaling. By automating routine tasks, you free up resources that can be redirected toward other growth opportunities.

Technology can support scaling in various ways:
- Automation: Automate routine tasks like email marketing, invoicing, or customer follow-ups.
- CRM Systems: Use CRM software to manage customer relationships and maintain personalized interactions.
- Data Analytics: Analyze customer data to make informed decisions, refine your marketing, and identify growth areas.

By leveraging technology, you create a business that's more responsive, efficient, and capable of handling an increase in customers or sales.

Expanding Your Reach Through Marketing and Branding

As you prepare to scale, one of the most effective ways to fuel growth is through strategic marketing. Expanding your reach requires getting your brand in front of new customers, building credibility, and creating a consistent message that resonates with your target audience.

Sarah, the owner of a custom jewelry business, wanted to grow beyond her local market. She invested in building a strong online presence, creating a website with high-quality photos and detailed descriptions of her jewelry pieces. She also launched an Instagram campaign, showcasing her products and partnering with influencers who shared her aesthetic and values. By tapping into social media and influencer marketing, Sarah reached thousands of new customers outside her local area, dramatically increasing her sales.

Sarah's marketing strategy illustrates the importance of building a strong brand presence when scaling. Effective marketing reaches new customers, builds trust, and creates a loyal following. When planning your marketing strategy for scaling, consider the following:

- Social Media: Use social platforms to share your brand story and showcase your products or services.

- Content Marketing: Create valuable content, such as blogs, videos, or guides, that establishes your expertise.

- Influencer Partnerships: Collaborate with influencers to expand your reach and build credibility with new audiences.

- Paid Advertising: Use targeted ads on platforms like Facebook, Instagram, and Google to attract potential customers.

Marketing isn't just about increasing sales; it's about creating a brand that people trust and feel connected to. When your brand resonates with customers, scaling becomes a natural progression rather than a forced push.

Building a Team that Supports Growth

Scaling isn't something you can do alone. As your business grows, you'll need to build a team that can support your vision and handle the increased workload. This often involves hiring strategically, finding the right talent, and creating a company culture that fosters productivity and innovation.

Marco, the founder of a digital marketing agency, started as a one-person operation. As demand for his services grew, he knew he needed a team to help him manage clients and execute campaigns. But rather than hiring full-time employees immediately, Marco began by working with freelancers and contractors. This allowed him to scale at a manageable pace, hiring additional support as he secured more clients.

Eventually, Marco transitioned to hiring full-time staff, creating a core team of specialists in areas like content marketing, social media, and SEO. By building a team that shared his values and goals, Marco was able to scale his agency and take on more significant clients, leading to a considerable increase in profits.

Building a team doesn't necessarily mean hiring a large staff. You can start small and bring on talent as needed. What's most important is finding people who align with your business values and can contribute to your growth.

## Focusing on Customer Retention

While attracting new customers is essential for growth, retaining existing customers can be even more valuable. Loyal customers not only provide repeat business but also act as advocates for your brand, helping you reach new audiences through word of mouth. Focusing on customer retention allows you to grow sustainably, increasing profitability without having to constantly spend on acquiring new customers.

Tom, the owner of a boutique coffee roastery, understood the value of customer loyalty. He created a subscription model, offering customers a monthly delivery of their favorite coffee blends. To further enhance customer satisfaction, he sent personalized notes with each order and offered exclusive discounts to subscribers. Tom's retention strategy led to steady revenue growth and a community of loyal customers who regularly referred new clients to his business.

By prioritizing customer retention, you can create a stable revenue stream that supports scaling.

Strategies for retaining customers include loyalty programs, personalized communication, and regular engagement through email or social media. Remember, it's often easier and more cost-effective to retain an existing customer than to acquire a new one.

## Using Financial Planning to Fund Growth

Scaling requires capital, whether it's for hiring staff, investing in technology, or expanding your marketing efforts. Having a financial plan is crucial to ensure that your growth is sustainable and that you're not overextending yourself. Many businesses fail because they grow too quickly without the financial resources to support expansion.

Lisa, the owner of a successful catering company, wanted to expand her services to corporate clients. She knew this would require purchasing additional equipment and hiring more staff. Rather than taking on high-interest debt, Lisa created a financial plan that allowed her to reinvest a portion of her profits back into her business. She also sought out a small business grant and used a line of credit with favorable terms.

Lisa's careful approach to financial planning helped her scale without jeopardizing her company's stability. As you plan for growth, consider creating a budget for scaling activities, seeking low-interest funding options, or reinvesting profits to fund your expansion.

Setting Key Performance Indicators (KPIs) to Measure Growth

To ensure that your scaling efforts are on track, it's essential to set Key Performance Indicators (KPIs) that measure your progress. KPIs help you track whether your strategies are working and identify areas that may need adjustment. Metrics like customer acquisition cost, profit margins, customer lifetime value, and revenue growth rate can provide insights into the health of your business.

Mike, the owner of an online fitness coaching business

, used KPIs to monitor his growth. By tracking metrics like monthly revenue, client retention, and customer satisfaction scores, he was able to identify which areas of his business were performing well and where he needed to make changes. This data-driven approach allowed Mike to make informed decisions, scaling his business strategically and effectively.

By setting clear KPIs, you can stay focused on your goals and ensure that each step you take contributes to your growth. Regularly reviewing these metrics allows you to adapt your strategy as needed, ensuring sustainable and profitable growth.

Scaling for Long-Term Success

Scaling a business for significant profit isn't a quick or easy process, but with the right strategies, it's entirely achievable. By focusing on building a solid foundation, creating a scalable model, leveraging technology, expanding your reach, and building a supportive team, you set your business up for sustainable growth. With each step, keep your customers at the heart of your efforts, prioritize financial planning, and monitor your progress through KPIs.

As you scale, remember that growth is a journey, not a destination.

# CHAPTER 7

## Leveraging the Power of Networking

Networking is often referred to as one of the most valuable skills in business, and for good reason. It's the relationships you build that can open doors, provide support, and lead you to opportunities you may have never discovered on your own. Yet, many people underestimate the power of networking or, worse, misunderstand it as merely transactional. True networking is about building meaningful connections, giving as much as you receive, and creating a foundation of trust.

In this chapter, we'll explore the principles of effective networking, the art of cultivating valuable relationships, and practical strategies to help you expand your network in ways that support your financial journey. From building rapport with industry leaders to engaging with your peers, the insights here will show you how to leverage the power of networking to reach your first million and beyond.

Understanding the Power of Networking

Networking is often misunderstood as superficial small talk or simply "collecting contacts." In reality, networking is about fostering relationships that are rooted in shared interests, mutual respect, and value. Successful networking goes beyond a single introduction or exchange of business cards; it involves genuine interest, ongoing communication, and creating ways to help one another.

Consider David, an entrepreneur who started a small tech company. Early on, David believed that the best way to grow his business was through hard work alone. But as he navigated the competitive tech industry, he quickly learned that the connections he made could be just as important as his skills. He began attending tech conferences and networking events, not with the intention of getting something, but to listen, learn, and offer help to others.

David's mindset shift from "getting" to "giving" helped him develop a strong network. He met mentors who offered him valuable advice, connected with peers who became collaborators, and even found a few investors who were impressed by his passion and commitment. His journey demonstrates that networking isn't just a one-time activity; it's an ongoing process that builds over time, creating a web of connections that can support your growth and goals.

The Foundation of Valuable Networking: Giving Before Receiving

One of the most effective approaches to networking is to focus on giving before receiving. When you approach networking with an attitude of generosity, you create goodwill, establish trust, and often gain the respect and appreciation of others.

Sarah, a young graphic designer, adopted this approach early in her career. Instead of viewing networking events as opportunities to promote herself, she saw them as chances to help others. At design meet-ups, she offered free advice to other creatives, shared resources, and volunteered her time for community projects. Over time, people came to know Sarah as someone who was genuinely invested in helping others. She built a strong reputation, and when her peers needed graphic design work or referrals, Sarah was the first person they thought of.

Sarah's story highlights that networking isn't about pushing your own agenda—it's about creating connections through mutual support. By helping others achieve their goals, you naturally build a network of people who are invested in your success.

Strategies to Give in Networking:
- Share Your Knowledge: Offer valuable advice, resources, or insights.
- Introduce Connections: Help others by connecting them with people in your network.

- Volunteer Your Time: Contribute to community or industry events.
- Celebrate Others' Success: Show genuine support for your peers' achievements.

Networking is most powerful when it's driven by authentic, supportive relationships. The people who value you for who you are and what you bring to the table are the ones who will be your most loyal advocates.

Creating and Cultivating Your Inner Circle

Your network doesn't have to be vast to be valuable. Building a solid "inner circle" of trusted connections is often more beneficial than amassing a large number of casual contacts. This inner circle can consist of mentors, peers, and collaborators who understand your goals, share your values, and support your journey.

Alex, a marketing consultant, recognized the importance of a close-knit network early in his career. He sought out a few experienced mentors and developed close relationships with colleagues he respected. His inner circle became a sounding board for his ideas, a source of encouragement during challenging times, and a well of referrals for new clients. By focusing on quality over quantity, Alex's network had a profound impact on his professional growth and profitability.

Building an inner circle is about choosing people who inspire and challenge you. This group of trusted connections can offer constructive feedback, open doors to new opportunities, and provide support through the highs and lows of your financial journey.

**How to Build Your Inner Circle:**

- Identify People Who Share Your Values: Look for individuals who align with your ethics and goals.
- Prioritize Quality: Focus on building deep, meaningful relationships rather than superficial contacts.
- Stay Connected: Regularly communicate and catch up with your inner circle to keep the bond strong.
- Offer and Seek Support: Be there for your circle, and don't hesitate to reach out when you need advice.

Your inner circle acts as your core network, grounding you in your goals and helping you stay focused on your path to financial freedom.

**Developing a Diverse Network**

While your inner circle is your core support system, a diverse network can broaden your perspective and expose you to new opportunities. A diverse network includes people from different industries, backgrounds, and experiences. This variety can provide you with unique insights, fresh ideas, and unexpected opportunities.

Rachel, an entrepreneur in the food industry, understood the value of a diverse network. In addition to connecting with people in her field, she reached out to individuals in tech, finance, and marketing. These connections helped her think creatively about her business. For example, a conversation with a software developer led her to implement a customer loyalty app, which boosted her sales significantly. Similarly, a connection in finance helped her navigate funding options, ultimately leading her to secure a loan with favorable terms.

By building a diverse network, Rachel gained insights and opportunities that she may not have found within her industry alone. Her experience shows that diversity in your network can spark innovation and open doors in unexpected ways.

Tips for Building a Diverse Network:
- Attend Cross-Industry Events: Explore conferences and workshops outside your field.
- Join Different Groups: Participate in organizations, meet-ups, or social groups with a variety of people.

- Seek Out Different Perspectives: Engage with individuals from different cultures, industries, and backgrounds.

- Be Open to Learning: Approach diverse connections with a willingness to learn from their experiences.

A diverse network enriches your knowledge, offers new perspectives, and expands the possibilities for collaboration and growth.

The Power of Mentorship and Learning from Experience

Mentorship is one of the most powerful elements of a network. A mentor can provide you with guidance, share their experiences, and help you navigate challenges on your path to financial freedom. Finding a mentor isn't about finding someone to do the work for you; it's about learning from someone who has already walked the path you're on.

Jared, a small business owner, credits his financial success to the mentorship of Rob, an experienced entrepreneur in his industry. Rob shared his own mistakes and successes with Jared, offering advice on everything from budgeting to hiring. This guidance helped Jared avoid costly pitfalls and make smarter decisions. With Rob's mentorship, Jared scaled his business more effectively, reaching his first million in revenue faster than he expected.

Mentors can provide valuable insights, open doors, and connect you with other resources within their network. The relationship is mutually beneficial, with mentors often finding fulfillment in helping others succeed.

How to Find and Engage with Mentors:
- Look for People You Admire: Seek mentors whose values and achievements align with your goals.
- Show Appreciation: Respect their time and express genuine gratitude for their guidance.
- Stay Engaged: Maintain regular communication and provide updates on your progress.
- Be a Mentor in Return: Give back by mentoring others who are on their own journeys.

Mentorship is a powerful force for growth. Learning from someone who has experienced similar challenges can accelerate your progress and deepen your understanding of the path ahead.

Networking in the Digital Age

In today's digital world, networking is no longer limited to in-person events. Social media, professional platforms like LinkedIn, and online communities offer new avenues to connect with people worldwide.

Online networking can be just as valuable as traditional methods, allowing you to reach a wider audience and engage with individuals you may never meet in person.

Emma, a freelance writer, built a successful business almost entirely through online networking. She joined writing groups, participated in Twitter chats, and engaged with influencers in her field on LinkedIn. By consistently showing up, sharing valuable content, and engaging with others, Emma developed a strong online presence. Her network provided referrals, freelance opportunities, and collaborations that helped her grow her income substantially.

Digital networking requires a different approach but can be incredibly effective. With the right strategies, you can build meaningful relationships online that have a tangible impact on your financial goals.

Tips for Effective Online Networking:
- Be Consistent: Engage regularly on social media platforms to stay visible in your industry.
- Add Value: Share insights, provide feedback, and offer support to others.
- Be Authentic: Genuine connections online are built through honesty and transparency.

- Follow Up: Take the time to follow up with people you connect with online to keep the relationship strong.

By embracing digital networking, you can reach a broader audience and build relationships that support your goals, even from a distance.

Leveraging Your Network for Financial Growth

Once you've built a network of valuable connections, it's important to understand how to leverage it effectively. Networking isn't just about who you know; it's about how you nurture those relationships to create mutual benefits. Your network can help you find

new clients, investors, collaborators, or even mentors to guide you further.

As you continue on your journey to financial freedom, remember that your network is a dynamic asset. The connections you make can provide support, open doors, and help you overcome obstacles. Cultivate these relationships with respect, gratitude, and a commitment to adding value, and your network will be a powerful force for growth, bringing you closer to achieving your first million.

Finding Mentors and Learning from Successful Individuals

Mentorship is a powerful catalyst on the road to financial success. When you find the right mentor, you gain access to a wealth of experience, insights, and guidance that can fast-track your progress and help you avoid common mistakes. Many people who achieve significant financial success credit mentors as a pivotal part of their journey. Learning from someone who has been in your shoes and successfully navigated the path to wealth can make a substantial difference in your own efforts to reach financial freedom.

However, finding a mentor isn't always straightforward. The key is to be intentional, proactive, and genuine in your search, recognizing that mentorship is a two-way relationship where respect and reciprocity are essential. This section explores the importance of mentorship, how to approach potential mentors, and ways to make the most of their guidance.

## Why Mentorship Matters?

A good mentor acts as both a guide and a role model, offering real-world insights that books, courses, or articles may not provide. They can help you see potential blind spots in your plans, introduce you to valuable contacts, and motivate you during challenging times. Mentors often share hard-earned wisdom that can save you from costly mistakes, giving you a significant advantage.

Take the example of Jordan, who started his own digital marketing agency with little more than an idea and determination. Early in his career, Jordan sought out a mentor who had already achieved success in the industry. This mentor helped Jordan avoid rookie errors, guided him on pricing and client negotiations, and encouraged him to stay resilient during slow business periods. Thanks to this mentorship, Jordan's agency grew faster and more sustainably than it might have if he had tried to do everything on his own.

## Where to Find Mentors?

Mentors can be found in various settings, from professional networks to unexpected personal connections. Here are some of the most effective places to seek out mentors:

1. Industry Events and Conferences: Events where professionals gather are ideal for finding mentors. Attendees are often open to sharing knowledge and connecting with motivated newcomers. Approach them respectfully, show curiosity, and ask thoughtful questions that demonstrate your interest.

2. Networking Groups and Organizations: Many professional associations offer mentorship programs or foster environments where experienced individuals are willing to guide newcomers. Joining industry organizations or community groups can help you meet potential mentors who align with your goals.

3. Social Media and Professional Platforms: Platforms like LinkedIn and Twitter allow you to follow and engage with industry leaders. Start by commenting on their posts, sharing their insights, and gradually building rapport. Direct messaging should be respectful and demonstrate genuine interest in their work and career.

4. Online Learning Communities: Some online courses or educational communities have dedicated mentorship programs or communities where mentors actively engage with students. These environments can create natural mentor-mentee relationships that are driven by shared interests and goals.

5. Referrals: Sometimes, the best mentors come through mutual connections. Let people in your existing network know that you're looking for mentorship, and they may be able to connect you with someone who is willing and capable of helping.

6. Within Your Workplace or Industry: If you're employed, you might find mentorship from senior

colleagues or industry veterans. These individuals often have a vested interest in seeing you succeed and may be willing to share their experiences with you.

Approaching Potential Mentors

Once you've identified someone you admire, reaching out in the right way is crucial. Many successful people are busy, so it's important to approach potential mentors thoughtfully and respectfully. Here are some guidelines:

1. Do Your Research: Learn about the potential mentor's background, values, and achievements before reaching out. Being knowledgeable about their career shows that you're genuinely interested and have put thought into why they'd be a good mentor for you.

2. Show Sincerity and Respect: In your initial contact, be clear, concise, and respectful of their time. Express why you admire them and how their journey resonates with your own aspirations. Authenticity is key; don't embellish or exaggerate.

3. Ask for a Small Commitment: Instead of asking for a formal, long-term mentorship, request a brief meeting or coffee chat. A short conversation feels more manageable and less intimidating for both you and your potential mentor. This initial conversation can naturally lead to further interactions.

4. Demonstrate Your Willingness to Learn: People enjoy mentoring those who are proactive and open to learning. Express a few specific areas where you seek their insights, but avoid asking for advice that you could easily find elsewhere. Show that you're committed to applying their guidance in practical ways.

5. Offer Something in Return: Even if you're just starting out, think about what you can offer in return. This could be as simple as sharing relevant industry news, offering feedback, or helping them with minor tasks that align with your skills.

6. Be Patient and Respectful of Boundaries: Remember that mentorship is a relationship, and relationships take time to grow. Don't pressure them to take on a mentorship role immediately; let it develop naturally as you continue to engage and learn.

Learning from Mentors: Making the Most of Their Guidance

Once you've connected with a mentor, the next step is to make the most of the relationship. Here's how to maximize the benefits of mentorship:

1. Listen More Than You Speak: When you're with your mentor, be a good listener. Pay attention,

take notes, and resist the urge to share your own thoughts too quickly. The goal is to absorb as much of their experience and insight as possible.

2. Ask Thoughtful Questions: Prepare questions that go beyond surface-level inquiries. For example, instead of asking, "What should I do to grow my business?" ask, "What were some of the biggest challenges you faced in scaling your business, and how did you overcome them?" Thoughtful questions lead to deeper, more valuable discussions.

3. Take Action on Their Advice: A mentor's time is valuable, so showing that you're implementing their advice is one of the best ways to respect that time. If they suggest a particular strategy, try it out and let them know how it worked. Following through demonstrates commitment and encourages your mentor to invest further in your growth.

4. Reflect on Your Progress Regularly: Mentorship is a two-way process, and one of the most effective ways to grow from the relationship is to reflect on your own progress. Regularly review what you've learned from your mentor, apply it, and assess your results. This reflective practice makes you a more intentional learner.

5. Express Gratitude: Always show appreciation for your mentor's time, insights, and support. Send thank-

you notes, share your successes, and let them know the impact they've had on your journey. Gratitude reinforces the relationship and shows them that you value their contribution.

6. Know When to Move On: Mentorship relationships sometimes evolve over time, and that's okay. As you grow, you might find that your needs change. When that happens, respectfully acknowledge the shift and, if appropriate, express your gratitude for the support they provided. Transitioning gracefully can help you maintain a positive relationship for years to come.

Case Study: The Power of Mentorship on the Path to Financial Freedom

Lily, an aspiring entrepreneur, dreamed of building her own fashion brand but lacked industry experience. She reached out to Janet, a successful designer with decades of experience in the fashion industry, after attending one of Janet's lectures. Lily was respectful, direct, and open about her ambitions, asking if Janet could spare a few minutes to chat about the industry.

Impressed by Lily's determination, Janet agreed to a brief meeting, which grew into an informal mentorship. Janet offered Lily guidance on everything from supply chain management to branding. She also shared her own experiences, both the successes and the setbacks, allowing Lily to learn from her mistakes without making the same ones herself. Over time, Janet even introduced Lily to some of her contacts, helping her build a network that led to funding opportunities and critical partnerships.

Lily's fashion brand launched successfully, and she credits Janet's mentorship for making her journey smoother and more manageable. With her mentor's help, Lily was able to scale her business, meet market demands, and achieve financial stability more quickly than she had initially imagined.

Final Thoughts: The Long-Term Impact of Mentorship on Financial Success

Mentorship is a powerful resource on the journey to financial freedom. Mentors offer a guiding hand through the complexities of business and finance, giving you insights that save time, energy, and money. Remember that finding the right mentor and building that relationship takes time, but the rewards can be transformative.

As you continue building your path to financial freedom, seek out individuals who inspire you, and don't hesitate to approach them with sincerity and respect. A mentor can be one of the most valuable assets on your journey to achieving your first million, providing support and wisdom that will last a lifetime.

## Making Connections that Lead to Financial Opportunities

Building a network is more than simply meeting people—it's about creating meaningful connections that can unlock doors to financial opportunities you might never have found on your own. Networking is often described as an "invisible asset" in achieving financial freedom. But unlike material assets, relationships are built over time, through authentic exchanges, trust, and a genuine desire to support one another.

Let's look at how Daniel, a young graphic designer with big ambitions but limited funds, leveraged connections to transform his career.

Daniel had been freelancing for a couple of years, mostly taking on small projects that kept the lights on but didn't exactly lead to the big paychecks he dreamed of. He knew he had potential but was struggling to get in front of the kinds of clients who could make a real impact on his financial life. One evening, he attended a networking event in the city's creative sector. Though he was nervous about approaching strangers, he forced himself to go, armed with his portfolio and a friendly smile.

As he made his way through the crowded room, Daniel met Claire, an established marketing consultant with a deep network of business contacts. Claire had been in the industry for over a decade and had a reputation for helping brands make big impressions. When Daniel introduced himself, Claire was polite but reserved. She likely met many young professionals eager for opportunities, so Daniel knew he needed to stand out. He decided to ask her about her work instead of pitching his own skills.

"Could you tell me about one of your favorite projects?" Daniel asked. Claire's face brightened, and she began sharing a story about a major brand overhaul she'd managed. Her eyes lit up with passion as she described the creative process, the challenges, and the satisfaction of seeing the results.

Listening carefully, Daniel realized he could learn a lot from Claire, so he continued to ask thoughtful questions. Claire noticed his genuine curiosity, and by the end of their conversation, she was curious about him too. When Daniel shared his portfolio, highlighting a project he'd recently completed, Claire was impressed by his eye for detail and fresh approach.

A week later, Claire reached out. She had a client who needed a brand refresh and thought Daniel's style might be a perfect fit. What started as a casual conversation led to a new client, and as it turned out, that client referred him to three others. Within six months, Daniel was working consistently, his income doubled, and he was building a reputation as a reliable, talented designer.

Identifying and Nurturing Connections

Daniel's story shows the power of forming connections that feel genuine and mutual. When you approach networking from a place of curiosity and value, people respond more openly. Here are some principles to remember when building relationships that could lead to financial opportunities:

1. Be Genuinely Interested: People can sense when someone is only interested in what they can gain. When you're genuinely interested in others' work and success, you lay a foundation for trust and respect. Show enthusiasm for their achievements, ask questions, and engage sincerely. When people feel valued, they're more likely to reciprocate.

2. Look for Synergies, Not Just Gains: Networking isn't about getting something from someone—it's about seeing how you can collaborate or support each other's goals. When you approach connections with this mindset, you build a network that's rich with

potential because it's founded on mutual benefit, not one-sided transactions.

3. Be Patient and Consistent: Connections rarely lead to opportunities overnight. Like any relationship, professional connections take time to mature. Stay in touch with people you admire, share industry news, and check in periodically. Consistency is key; it keeps you on their radar and shows that you're invested in the relationship over the long term.

Connections That Lead to Financial Opportunities: Case Study of Leah

Leah, a software developer, worked in a small tech company. She wanted to start her own tech consulting business, but she was unsure where to begin. She attended tech conferences and local startup events in her free time, but her goal was always to build genuine connections, not just collect business cards.

At one event, Leah met James, the CEO of a successful app development firm. Rather than launching into a pitch about her own abilities, Leah asked James about his journey—how he started his company, the challenges he faced, and his vision for the future. Leah found James's journey inspiring and later followed up with a message thanking him for the conversation.

Over the next few months, Leah stayed in touch with James, sharing insights about emerging technologies she was experimenting with, occasionally inviting him to industry talks, and even introducing him to people in her network who could be beneficial for his projects. She gave value first, without expecting anything in return.

A few months later, James contacted Leah with a proposal: his company needed a consulting partner for a new project. He liked her technical knowledge and trusted her character, having seen her consistent professionalism and interest in adding value. This project became the first big contract of Leah's independent consulting career, and through James's recommendation, she gained several other high-profile clients.

Leah's story illustrates that financial opportunities from networking often come indirectly, through the trust you build over time. Instead of pushing for an immediate reward, Leah's approach emphasized patience, respect, and adding value. This approach didn't just lead to one contract—it laid the groundwork for a lasting professional relationship.

Turning Connections Into Opportunities

Turning connections into financial opportunities doesn't happen by luck; it's about nurturing relationships intentionally. Here are a few ways to create opportunities from your network:

1. Stay Top of Mind: Reach out periodically to connections, even if there's no immediate reason to do so. A simple "hello" or sharing an article that might interest them keeps you in their thoughts without any pressure.

2. Add Value Before Asking for Help: If you see an opportunity to introduce them to someone valuable, help with a small task, or share resources, take it. Offering value before asking for anything builds goodwill and establishes you as someone who is a positive presence in their network.

3. Ask for Advice, Not Favors: People enjoy sharing their expertise and feel honored when asked for advice. Instead of directly asking for job leads or funding, approach them with questions about their experience and wisdom. Often, these conversations naturally lead to opportunities as they think of ways to support you.

4. Share Your Goals: Once trust has been built, share your ambitions and what you're working on. By expressing your aspirations, you make it easier for others to connect you to opportunities that align with your goals.

5. Follow Through on Their Recommendations: If a contact gives you advice or a referral, act on it. This shows that you value their input and reinforces their willingness to support you in the future.

## Real-Life Example: The Ripple Effect of Networking

Consider Alicia, who worked in marketing and wanted to start a social media consulting agency. Through her network, she was introduced to David, a successful entrepreneur in a different industry. David was intrigued by Alicia's ideas and introduced her to his own contacts who needed help with social media strategy.

Through this connection, Alicia gained her first clients, but the real opportunity came when one of those clients connected her to a popular influencer. The influencer, impressed with Alicia's expertise, hired her for a year-long contract and recommended her services to other brands.

The ripple effect of David's initial introduction led to Alicia building her own agency with multiple high-profile clients. Alicia's experience highlights the power of networking when approached with authenticity. Because she delivered quality work, the initial connection multiplied, creating a steady stream of clients who trusted her based on the endorsements of others.

Final Thoughts: Building a Network of Financial Opportunity

Networking can be one of the most powerful tools in your journey to financial freedom. Remember that successful networking is a combination of building trust, showing up consistently, and genuinely investing in the people around you. When approached with sincerity and a commitment to mutual benefit, networking doesn't just connect you to people—it connects you to financial possibilities, new ventures, and a lifetime of professional growth.

So, as you continue on your path toward financial freedom, focus on making connections that matter. By giving first, being genuinely interested, and staying consistent, you'll find yourself surrounded by a network that not only enriches your career but also leads you to the financial success you've envisioned.

# CHAPTER 8

## Tax Efficiency and Legal Considerations

In the journey toward financial freedom, mastering tax efficiency and understanding legal considerations are essential tools. It's one thing to make money; it's another to keep it. For most people striving toward their first million, taxes represent one of the largest expenses they'll encounter. Navigating the complexities of tax planning and wealth management can be daunting, but with the right strategies and insights, you can keep more of your earnings, protect your wealth, and create a legally sound path to financial freedom.

Let's delve into how tax efficiency and legal planning can help you unlock the full potential of your income, illustrated through stories of those who've leveraged smart strategies to retain more of what they earn.

Why Tax Efficiency Matters: The Story of Mark

Mark, a software developer from Texas, always assumed taxes were a fixed part of life. He saw taxes as unavoidable and paid them without much thought.

Each year, a sizable portion of his hard-earned income vanished before it reached his pocket, disappearing into federal, state, and local taxes. But as Mark advanced in his career and started taking on freelance work, his tax burden increased, and he found himself frustrated by how much of his income was going to the government.

One day, while having lunch with an old friend, he mentioned his frustrations. His friend, a business owner, laughed and said, "You're not alone. But you know, there's a way to keep more of your money." Mark was intrigued. His friend explained how she worked with a tax advisor who specialized in helping small business owners, freelancers, and professionals maximize tax efficiency. With some skepticism but also a glimmer of hope, Mark decided to give tax planning a shot.

The next tax season, he sat down with a certified tax advisor. Together, they reviewed his finances and work structure, considering deductions he had never realized were available to him, such as his home office, business travel expenses, and professional software subscriptions. They explored strategies for maximizing his retirement contributions and identified opportunities to defer income.

For Mark, this was a revelation. Instead of simply paying his taxes and moving on, he began to actively plan his finances with tax efficiency in mind. By the end of that year, he had saved nearly $15,000—money he used to further invest in his retirement and increase his emergency fund. Tax efficiency had become more than just a strategy; it was a way to directly improve his financial future.

The Fundamentals of Tax Efficiency

Mark's story illustrates that tax efficiency doesn't require a business degree or a complex financial plan — it simply requires knowledge, strategy, and a proactive approach. Tax efficiency is about reducing your tax burden legally and maximizing the amount you can keep to grow your wealth.

For anyone aspiring to financial freedom, here are some fundamental tax concepts:

1. Tax Deductions and Credits: Deductions reduce your taxable income, meaning you owe less tax. Credits, on the other hand, directly reduce the amount of tax you owe. Understanding and maximizing deductions (like mortgage interest, charitable donations, or business expenses) and tax credits (like education or renewable energy credits) is essential.

2. Tax-Advantaged Accounts: Certain accounts, such as 401(k)s, IRAs, Health Savings Accounts

(HSAs), and 529 college savings plans, allow you to save money tax-free or tax-deferred. These accounts are not just for saving—they're powerful tools for reducing your taxable income.

3. Capital Gains Tax: When you sell an asset like stocks or real estate, the profit you earn is subject to capital gains tax. Long-term investments (held over a year) are typically taxed at a lower rate than short-term gains, so it's wise to hold on to assets longer whenever possible.

4. Deferment and Income Splitting: Strategies such as deferring income to a lower-income year, or splitting income with family members in lower tax brackets, can be beneficial in managing your tax burden.

5. Entity Structure for Business Owners: Choosing the right structure for your business—such as an LLC, S-corporation, or partnership—can offer significant tax advantages. Each structure has its own set of benefits and requirements, so understanding which is best for you can optimize your tax efficiency.

A Practical Example: Tax-Advantaged Accounts and Compound Growth

Consider Jenna, an HR consultant who worked as an independent contractor. She was in her 30s, loved her job, but hated the high tax burden. Jenna's accountant recommended maximizing her contributions to a **SEP-IRA** (Simplified Employee Pension Individual Retirement Account), a retirement account designed for self-employed individuals and small business owners.

By contributing a significant portion of her income into a tax-advantaged account, Jenna reduced her taxable income by thousands of dollars each year. Over time, the money in her **SEP-IRA** grew through compounding returns, meaning her savings not only avoided taxes in the present but also grew tax-free until retirement. When Jenna turned 60, her initial contributions had compounded to several hundred thousand dollars, securing her financial future.

The lesson here is that maximizing contributions to tax-advantaged accounts is a powerful way to shelter income, create a buffer against taxes, and use compounding to grow your wealth significantly.

Leveraging Legal Structures: Maria's Journey as a Business Owner

Maria owned a successful event-planning business. As the company grew, she became aware of how her current tax setup was holding her back. At that point, she was operating as a sole proprietor, which meant her business income was taxed at her personal income rate.

After consulting with a tax advisor, Maria restructured her business as an S-corporation. This change allowed her to pay herself a reasonable salary and take the rest of her profits as distributions, which were taxed at a lower rate than regular income. The S-corporation structure also provided Maria with additional tax-deductible expenses, such as health insurance premiums and retirement contributions for her employees.

The outcome? Maria was able to retain an additional 20% of her earnings each year. The savings were reinvested into her business, which enabled it to grow even faster. Maria's experience shows how choosing the right legal structure can provide tax advantages and fuel further growth.

Practical Tips for Tax Efficiency

1. Work with a Tax Professional: The complexity of tax law requires guidance from professionals who understand your unique situation. They can help you uncover deductions, credits, and strategies specific to your industry.

2. Keep Accurate Records: Maintaining meticulous records is essential for tax efficiency. This

includes receipts, invoices, and documentation for any expenses related to your business or investments. Proper record-keeping also reduces stress in the event of an audit.

3. Be Strategic with Investments: Understanding tax implications for each investment can save you thousands over time. For example, tax-efficient funds or tax-exempt bonds can reduce your tax burden while still allowing for growth.

4. Use Technology: There are many digital tools designed to help individuals and businesses track their expenses, monitor deductions, and simplify tax preparation. Investing in these tools can streamline your tax planning.

5. Stay Informed on Tax Law Changes: Tax laws change frequently, so staying updated on any shifts is critical. New laws can impact deductions, tax rates, and credits available to you, making it essential to adapt your strategies as the landscape evolves.

Legal Considerations: Protecting Your Wealth

As you accumulate wealth, legal considerations play an increasingly important role in protecting it. This includes asset protection, estate planning, and intellectual property.

1. Asset Protection: Safeguarding your assets through trusts, insurance, or legal structures protects your wealth against lawsuits or creditors. William, a doctor who invested in several real estate properties, chose to place each property in a separate LLC, which minimized his liability exposure. If one property encountered legal trouble, it would not threaten his entire portfolio.

2. Estate Planning: As you grow your wealth, planning for its distribution upon your passing becomes critical. Estate planning tools such as wills, trusts, and charitable donations ensure your wealth goes to your loved ones or causes you support, rather than being diminished by estate taxes.

3. Intellectual Property Protection: For those with businesses that depend on intellectual property, protecting your ideas through patents, copyrights, or trademarks can add tremendous value to your portfolio.

Lessons Learned: Tax Efficiency as a Key to Financial Freedom

Understanding tax efficiency and legal considerations can be transformative in your journey toward financial independence. When implemented thoughtfully, these strategies allow you to keep more of your earnings, invest in your future, and protect your wealth for the long term.

Consider Ryan, a marketing executive who initially overlooked the impact taxes had on his earnings. After actively learning about tax planning and asset protection, he set up a retirement account, structured his side business as an LLC, and created a simple trust. Ten years later, Ryan's tax-saving efforts compounded into additional investments, which grew to over $200,000—an amount he wouldn't have achieved had he paid higher taxes year after year.

Achieving financial freedom isn't just about how much you earn; it's about how much you keep, grow, and protect. In understanding the art of tax efficiency and the wisdom of legal planning, you're building a strong foundation on which to grow your wealth without unnecessary losses.

As you progress toward your first million, make tax efficiency and legal considerations a core part of your strategy. With these tools, you're not just building wealth—you're preserving and protecting it, ensuring that each dollar works as hard as you do on the journey to financial freedom.

In the pursuit of financial freedom, reaching your first million is an exciting milestone, but one key principle often overlooked is safeguarding the wealth you've worked so hard to accumulate. Setting up legal protections is like fortifying a castle: once you've built something valuable, it's critical to establish defenses that prevent unexpected events from causing irreparable harm. This chapter delves into the world of asset protection, showing you practical steps, real-world stories, and the essential legal tools you can use to keep your wealth safe.

The Wake-Up Call: James's Story

James was a small business owner who had built his local contracting company from scratch. For years, he operated his business as a sole proprietor. When things were going well, he didn't think much about legal protections; his primary focus was on growth and bringing in more clients. But one day, everything changed when a former client filed a lawsuit claiming damages from an unfinished project.

The lawsuit blindsided James. Since he was operating as a sole proprietor, his personal assets— including his home, his retirement savings, and even his children's college fund—were all exposed. James fought hard, but the legal fees and eventual settlement took a massive toll on his finances. He had poured years of hard work into building his wealth, only to see it threatened in a matter of weeks. It was a painful but eye-opening experience.

Determined not to go through such an ordeal again, James decided to educate himself on asset protection. With the help of a financial advisor and a lawyer, he restructured his business, separating his personal finances from his business obligations. Through limited liability protections and trust setups, James took steps to ensure that his future earnings—and his family's security—would be shielded from legal risks.

James's story is a common one: people often don't realize how vulnerable their assets are until something goes wrong. By learning from his experience, we can see the importance of proactive asset protection and the benefits of setting up legal structures to defend what we've worked so hard to build.

### Understanding Asset Protection: Why It's Not Just for the Wealthy

Many people assume that asset protection is a strategy reserved for the ultra-wealthy or for large corporations. In reality, anyone who has accumulated even a modest level of wealth can benefit from basic asset protection measures. This protection becomes especially crucial as you start approaching significant financial milestones—such as your first million—where the impact of potential losses becomes greater.

At its core, asset protection is about creating a legal buffer between your personal assets and potential claims. By separating your assets from any risks or liabilities associated with your work or business activities, you're effectively building a shield around your wealth. Let's explore some practical steps you can take to protect your hard-earned assets and ensure they're there to serve your future.

1. Choosing the Right Business Structure: Limited Liability Companies (LLCs) and Corporations

If you run a business, the structure you choose can have a huge impact on your liability exposure. Sole proprietorships are simple and inexpensive to set up, but they leave you entirely exposed to personal liability. In contrast, forming a Limited Liability Company (LLC) or a corporation can separate your personal assets from those of the business.

Take the case of Samantha, a graphic designer who turned her freelance business into a thriving agency. Early on, Samantha realized that working as a sole proprietor left her exposed to any claims that might arise from her work. By setting up her business as an LLC, she established a legal distinction between her personal finances and her business. Should anything happen—a dissatisfied client or a dispute over contract terms—Samantha's personal savings and assets would be protected, as only the business's assets would be at risk.

Establishing a business entity like an LLC or S-Corp might involve upfront legal fees and paperwork, but the long-term security it provides is invaluable. As Samantha's example shows, an LLC or corporation offers a foundational level of asset protection that ensures personal security even in the face of business setbacks.

2. Shielding Assets with Trusts: Protecting Wealth for Future Generations

Trusts are one of the most powerful tools for protecting assets, especially when it comes to long-term wealth preservation. Essentially, a trust is a legal entity that holds assets on behalf of a beneficiary. By transferring ownership of assets into a trust, you can protect them from claims, creditors, and even estate taxes.

Laura, a successful consultant who had built a portfolio of real estate investments, knew she wanted to pass her wealth down to her children. However, she was worried that future legal claims, estate taxes, or other risks could diminish her legacy. To safeguard her assets, Laura established an irrevocable trust. By placing her properties and investments in the trust, she ensured that they would be protected from creditors, lawsuits, or potential estate taxes. Additionally, her children would receive the assets as outlined in the trust terms, giving her peace of mind that her family's financial future was secure.

Trusts come in different forms, each with unique benefits. Revocable trusts allow you to maintain control over assets but provide limited liability protection, while irrevocable trusts offer a stronger legal shield by transferring ownership of assets entirely. Setting up a trust involves legal guidance, but for those with a growing wealth base, it's an essential part of protecting wealth and securing it for future generations.

3. Using Insurance as a Protective Barrier

Sometimes, asset protection doesn't require complex legal structures but can be as simple as having the right insurance policies in place. Insurance acts as the first line of defense, covering unexpected risks without jeopardizing your core assets.

For instance, Tom was a real estate investor who had acquired several rental properties. Knowing that accidents, property damage, or tenant disputes could arise, he made sure to carry comprehensive liability insurance for each property. When a tenant accidentally injured himself on the property, Tom's insurance policy covered the medical expenses and legal fees, preventing him from dipping into his own funds or selling assets to cover the costs.

Insurance doesn't just apply to real estate. Business liability insurance, professional liability (also known as "errors and omissions") insurance, and even personal umbrella policies all serve as crucial tools in asset protection. For the relatively low cost of annual premiums, insurance provides invaluable peace of mind and a safety net that can save your wealth when the unexpected happens.

4. Homestead Exemptions and Protecting Your Primary Residence

For many people, their home is their most valuable asset, and there are ways to protect this crucial investment as well. A homestead exemption is a legal provision that protects the value of your primary residence from creditors or lawsuits, up to a certain limit, depending on the state.

Evelyn, a retired schoolteacher, owned her home outright. She was cautious about taking any unnecessary risks that might jeopardize her most valuable asset. By filing for a homestead exemption in her state, she ensured that, even if she faced a lawsuit or debt issue, her primary residence would remain protected. For Evelyn, this was a simple step that brought significant security.

Homestead exemptions are typically straightforward to apply for and provide an added layer of protection. Each state has different rules, so it's important to understand what's available in your area and make the necessary applications if you're eligible.

5. Intellectual Property Protection: Safeguarding Ideas and Innovations

For entrepreneurs, creatives, and business owners, intellectual property (IP) can be as valuable as physical assets. Patents, trademarks, copyrights, and trade secrets protect your unique ideas, products, and brands from being copied or misused by competitors.

Consider Aaron, an engineer who developed a unique software solution. By patenting his invention and securing copyrights for his software, he ensured that no other entity could legally replicate or distribute his work without his permission. Through these IP protections, Aaron not only created a lucrative licensing opportunity but also prevented potential competitors from undercutting his market.

Protecting intellectual property can involve initial legal expenses, but these protections are invaluable. A strong IP portfolio can become a powerful asset that generates income and retains value over time, enhancing the overall worth of your financial portfolio.

The Power of Proactive Protection

As these stories highlight, asset protection isn't just about amassing wealth—it's about taking steps to keep that wealth safe for yourself and future generations. Setting up legal protections requires forethought, guidance, and some upfront effort, but it's an investment in peace of mind that pays dividends over time.

Protecting your assets gives you the freedom to take calculated risks, knowing you have a secure foundation. It also safeguards your family's future, ensuring that the financial gains you've worked hard for are not at risk from unexpected events. Whether through legal structures, insurance, exemptions, or intellectual property, these protections allow you to focus on building wealth rather than worrying about losing it.

As you journey toward financial independence, remember that asset protection is more than just a safety measure—it's an empowering step that ensures your financial foundation is as strong as the wealth you're working to create.

For anyone striving toward financial freedom, taxes play a major role in how wealth accumulates—or slips away. The journey to retaining and growing wealth requires not only smart investments and steady saving habits but also a proactive approach to understanding and leveraging tax incentives. A strategic tax plan can be the difference between rapid financial growth and stagnation, helping you retain more of what you earn and reinvest it to fuel further growth.

A Lesson in Tax Savvy: Sarah's Strategy

Sarah was a young entrepreneur who had recently launched a successful e-commerce business. The demand for her unique, eco-friendly products grew quickly, and within a couple of years, she was generating six-figure revenues. But when tax season rolled around, Sarah was surprised by the size of her tax bill, realizing she had to pay out a substantial chunk of her profits.

Feeling overwhelmed by her tax burden, Sarah decided to learn more about tax incentives and strategies that could help her keep more of her hard-earned money. She soon discovered several key ways to use tax incentives to reduce her obligations and increase her wealth. With the help of an accountant, Sarah implemented several tactics that not only minimized her taxes but also gave her additional capital to reinvest in her business, leading to faster growth and higher profits.

Sarah's experience illustrates a powerful truth: effective tax management isn't just about avoiding losses; it's a powerful tool for wealth building. Let's dive into some specific ways tax incentives can work in your favor.

### 1. Business Deductions: Lowering Taxable Income While Building Your Brand

One of the first tax strategies Sarah's accountant taught her was the power of business deductions. By tracking and deducting expenses directly related to her business, Sarah could lower her taxable income, thereby reducing her overall tax bill. Everything from office supplies to marketing costs and travel expenses became deductions that helped lower her business's taxable income.

Take her marketing expenses as an example. Sarah wanted to grow her brand, and she'd been considering hiring a digital marketing team to help her reach a broader audience. Knowing that these expenses would be tax-deductible, she invested confidently, realizing she could both strengthen her brand and reduce her taxable income. By the time tax season arrived, Sarah's overall tax liability was significantly reduced, and her brand had grown immensely, thanks to the marketing efforts.

For anyone with a business or side hustle, understanding and leveraging business deductions can free up significant capital that would otherwise go to taxes. This capital can be reinvested, creating a cycle of growth and tax savings that fuels long-term wealth accumulation.

2. Retirement Accounts: Building Wealth with Tax-Advantaged Savings

Another crucial area Sarah learned about was tax-advantaged retirement accounts. Like many business owners, she had initially been so focused on her business that she hadn't thought about retirement planning. But her accountant explained the advantages of opening accounts like a **SEP-IRA** or a Solo 401(k), which would allow her to contribute pre-tax income, thereby lowering her taxable income.

Sarah began contributing a portion of her earnings to a **SEP-IRA**. This decision not only reduced her taxable income in the short term but also allowed her to invest her savings in a tax-deferred account, letting her wealth grow without the drag of yearly taxes.

For employees, traditional IRAs and employer-sponsored 401(k) accounts serve similar purposes, allowing individuals to put away pre-tax income for the future. By consistently contributing to these accounts, anyone can grow their wealth tax-free until withdrawal, creating a "snowball effect" that builds significant savings over time.

3. Capital Gains Tax: Strategies for Investing Wisely

One of the less obvious but powerful strategies Sarah learned about was managing her investments to minimize capital gains tax. Any time an investment is sold at a profit, capital gains tax is due on the earnings. However, Sarah's accountant explained that holding investments for over a year qualified them as long-term gains, which are taxed at a much lower rate than short-term gains.

Inspired, Sarah shifted her investment strategy to focus on long-term holds. She invested in a mix of stocks and mutual funds with a plan to hold them for several years, allowing her to benefit from lower tax rates on her gains. By doing this, she retained more of her investment returns, which she reinvested to grow her wealth further.

This approach to capital gains applies to anyone investing in stocks, bonds, or real estate. By planning around capital gains tax rates, investors can increase their overall returns, reinvesting the savings to grow their wealth with fewer tax obligations eating into their profits.

4. Real Estate Tax Advantages: Making Wealth Grow with Property Investments

Real estate is not just an asset that appreciates over time; it's also a powerful tax-sheltering tool. Sarah wasn't initially interested in real estate, but after hearing about the tax advantages, she decided to purchase a rental property with her savings. She soon discovered the many ways property investments could help her retain wealth.

First, she could depreciate the value of the property, a non-cash expense that lowered her taxable income without reducing her actual cash flow. This allowed her to offset rental income, meaning she paid less tax on her profits from the property. Additionally, when she made improvements—such as updating the kitchen or installing energy-efficient windows—these costs were deductible as well.

Through property ownership, Sarah realized that her rental income was largely shielded from taxes, and she could continue to build equity over time. Real estate investors around the world use these tax benefits to grow their portfolios, leveraging the savings to purchase additional properties, which generates even more passive income.

5. Health Savings Accounts (HSAs): A Triple Tax Advantage

Sarah didn't initially consider health savings accounts (HSAs) as a wealth-building tool, but she quickly learned they offered a unique, triple tax advantage: contributions are tax-deductible, growth within the account is tax-free, and withdrawals for qualified medical expenses are also tax-free.

She opened an HSA and contributed the maximum allowed amount, planning to use it for future health expenses. Because her contributions were tax-deductible, she reduced her current year's tax liability while allowing the account to grow without being taxed on the earnings. When the time came to use the funds for medical expenses, the withdrawals would be tax-free. This tax efficiency allowed Sarah to put more money toward other wealth-building efforts while securing her future healthcare needs.

HSAs are an excellent option for anyone with a high-deductible health insurance plan, offering tax-efficient savings that can grow significantly over time.

6. State Tax Incentives: Taking Advantage of Regional Opportunities

When Sarah decided to expand her business, she was considering several states with favorable business environments. Upon researching, she discovered that some states offered tax credits and incentives to encourage small business growth, including reduced property taxes, credits for hiring locally, and even grants for specific industries.

Sarah eventually expanded her business into a state that offered tax credits for eco-friendly businesses. This decision saved her thousands of dollars, which she reinvested into her business's sustainability initiatives. By aligning her expansion with state incentives, she not only saved on taxes but also built a brand reputation as an environmentally conscious business.

For anyone running a business, researching state-specific tax incentives can uncover opportunities to save, invest, and grow. These regional benefits can be a strategic advantage for long-term wealth accumulation.

Transforming Tax Strategy into Wealth Growth

Sarah's journey shows that effective tax planning goes far beyond paying less in taxes—it's about finding strategic opportunities to build, protect, and grow wealth. By leveraging deductions, tax-advantaged accounts, capital gains planning, real estate advantages, HSAs, and state-specific incentives, Sarah not only minimized her tax burden but created a plan that maximized her financial growth.

For those on the path to financial freedom, understanding tax incentives is like unlocking hidden doors to wealth accumulation. Each tax-saving opportunity adds another layer to your wealth, letting you retain more of what you earn and freeing up funds to fuel further growth. By building a proactive tax strategy, you're not just reducing your tax bill; you're creating a wealth-building plan that maximizes every dollar you earn, positioning yourself for a future of sustained financial freedom.

# CHAPTER 9

## Financial Resilience and Risk Management

When it comes to financial freedom, resilience is your hidden asset. Financial resilience isn't just about being prepared for tough times—it's the ability to adapt, recover, and even thrive when the unexpected occurs. Economic downturns, market shifts, and unforeseen crises are inevitable in the journey to building wealth. Yet, those who prepare for these fluctuations emerge stronger and more capable of reaching their financial goals. This chapter delves into the principles of financial resilience and risk management, showing how strategic planning and emotional readiness can safeguard your wealth and empower you to make steady progress, regardless of the economic climate.

The Story of Tom and Sarah: A Lesson in Financial Resilience

Tom and Sarah were two close friends who set out on similar paths to financial freedom. Both had well-paying jobs, both saved and invested consistently, and both had big dreams of financial independence. Tom invested most of his earnings in the stock market, placing high-risk bets that had the potential for high returns. He loved the thrill of investing in trending tech stocks and emerging sectors, confident that his bold moves would pay off.

Sarah, on the other hand, took a more diversified approach. She spread her investments across various asset classes, including stocks, bonds, and real estate, balancing her high-risk investments with safer options. She also built an emergency fund, a cash reserve she kept on hand for unexpected situations, and invested in insurance to protect herself from unforeseen risks.

Then came a market downturn that shook the economy. Stocks plummeted, companies cut jobs, and for many, the economic future looked bleak. Tom's portfolio took a huge hit, losing nearly half its value. The emotional stress took a toll on him as well; he panicked, sold his investments at a loss, and found himself back at square one.

Sarah's portfolio, on the other hand, was impacted but much less severely. Her diversified approach and cash reserves helped her weather the storm. She didn't need to sell her assets because she had enough in her emergency fund to get through the rough patch. By the time the market rebounded, she was not only back on track but had gained from the upswing because she stayed invested. Sarah's financial resilience allowed her to continue her journey toward financial freedom, while Tom had to start over, facing the hard lesson that high-risk strategies don't always lead to lasting wealth.

## Understanding Economic Cycles and Market Changes

To develop financial resilience, it's essential to understand economic cycles and how they can impact your wealth-building journey. The economy naturally goes through periods of growth, stability, and contraction, much like the changing seasons. During times of growth, employment rates are high, businesses expand, and the stock market often rises. However, this growth isn't sustainable forever. At some point, the economy reaches a peak and starts to contract, leading to a recession or downturn.

For anyone pursuing financial freedom, it's crucial to anticipate these changes and not be caught off-guard. Understanding that downturns are inevitable and preparing for them can protect you from panic and poor decision-making. While you can't control the market, you can control how prepared you are to weather its changes. Here are some strategies to build financial resilience that can help you prepare for both the highs and lows of the economy.

1. Build a Solid Emergency Fund

An emergency fund is the foundation of financial resilience. It's the buffer that allows you to handle unexpected expenses or temporary losses in income without dipping into your investments or accumulating debt. Most financial experts recommend having three to six months' worth of living expenses in an easily accessible account.

Imagine being able to weather a job loss, a medical emergency, or a sudden car repair without worrying about how to cover your bills. That's the peace of mind an emergency fund provides. Sarah, for instance, didn't have to sell her investments at a loss during the downturn because her emergency fund kept her covered. She could ride out the market's fluctuations, waiting for it to recover before making any moves.

Consider this fund a non-negotiable component of your financial plan. Place it in a high-yield savings account where it remains safe from market volatility but still earns a bit of interest.

2. Diversify Your Income Streams

Relying on a single income stream is a risk in itself, as it leaves you vulnerable to sudden shifts in that one source. Diversifying your income can mean investing in stocks, bonds, and real estate, but it also extends to having multiple sources of earnings, such as a side business or rental property.

Think about income diversification like this: if one stream dries up, others can still keep you afloat. Sarah, for instance, had income from her job, her real estate investment, and her diversified stock portfolio. This diversification not only provided her with multiple sources of cash flow but also distributed her risk. When her stock portfolio took a hit during the downturn, her rental income remained steady, helping her manage expenses without relying solely on her job.

To build resilience, think about how you can add more income sources to your life. A side business, freelance work, or investing in dividend-paying stocks can give you additional layers of financial security, making you less reliant on any single source of income.

3. Practice Responsible Debt Management

Debt can be both a tool and a trap. Used responsibly, it can help you leverage your finances to build wealth, but left unchecked, it can quickly become a burden that drains your financial resources.

Consider the story of Mike, a successful entrepreneur who leveraged loans to grow his business. However, he was careful not to take on more debt than he could handle. He tracked his cash flow meticulously, ensuring he could meet his debt payments even in lean months. When the economy slowed, Mike's conservative approach to debt kept his business stable, allowing him to weather the downturn without risking insolvency.

The key to managing debt effectively is understanding how much you can afford and creating a plan for repayment. Avoid high-interest consumer debt, such as credit card debt, and focus on "good debt" that contributes to your wealth, like a mortgage or a low-interest business loan. When you manage debt wisely, you minimize financial strain and increase your resilience in any economy.

4. Insurance as a Safety Net

Insurance is another critical aspect of financial resilience, yet many overlook it in their quest for financial freedom. Think of insurance as the safety net that protects you from worst-case scenarios. Health, life, disability, and even property insurance can shield you from massive expenses that would otherwise derail your financial plans.

Let's revisit Sarah. Her decision to invest in health and disability insurance proved invaluable. When she faced a minor health issue that required surgery, her insurance covered the bulk of the expenses, allowing her to focus on recovery rather than worry about costs. This proactive step ensured her savings and investments remained intact, reinforcing her financial stability.

Insurance doesn't eliminate risks, but it does mitigate their impact. It's an investment in your peace of mind and an essential component of any risk management strategy.

5. Embrace a Flexible Investment Strategy

When it comes to investing, flexibility is a cornerstone of resilience. A rigid, all-or-nothing approach to investing can backfire during market fluctuations. In contrast, a flexible strategy allows you to adapt to changing conditions, adjusting your portfolio as needed without panic.

Sarah adopted a diversified, balanced investment strategy, splitting her funds across stocks, bonds, and real estate. She maintained a balanced mix of growth-oriented stocks and more conservative assets like bonds, which provided stability during downturns. This flexibility meant she didn't need to panic-sell when stocks dropped; her bond investments and cash reserves buffered her portfolio, allowing her to ride out the storm.

For anyone investing, consider maintaining a balanced portfolio that suits your risk tolerance but includes a mix of assets. Staying flexible doesn't mean abandoning your goals—it means adjusting your approach when necessary to stay on track.

6. Develop an Adaptable Mindset

Financial resilience isn't just about money; it's about your mindset. An adaptable mindset is your greatest tool in navigating financial challenges. Recognize that setbacks are part of the journey, not the end of it. Resilient individuals don't dwell on losses; they focus on what can be learned and move forward with determination.

Take, for example, the story of Daniel, who lost his job during an economic downturn. Instead of panicking, he saw it as an opportunity to pivot. He leveraged his skills to start a consulting business, working on freelance projects to support himself. Within a year, he was not only back on his feet but thriving, earning more than he did at his previous job. His ability to adapt and turn a setback into an opportunity showcased the power of resilience.

By fostering an adaptable mindset, you're better prepared to handle economic downturns, market changes, and personal setbacks. This mental resilience allows you to keep pushing toward your financial goals, even in uncertain times.

The Power of Financial Resilience in Your Journey to Financial Freedom

Financial resilience and risk management are about more than preparing for economic downturns —they are fundamental to achieving and sustaining financial freedom. Resilience allows you to stay the course when times are tough, while risk management ensures you don't take unnecessary gambles that could jeopardize your goals.

As you continue on your path to financial freedom, remember that resilience isn't built in a day. It's cultivated through strategic planning, disciplined habits, and a forward-thinking mindset. Whether it's building an emergency fund, diversifying your income, or practicing debt management, each step you take toward financial resilience reinforces your ability to overcome obstacles and unlock your first million.

This journey isn't only about accumulating wealth —it's about becoming a financially empowered individual who can withstand and thrive in any economic climate. When you build financial resilience, you're not just preparing for the next downturn; you're preparing for a lifetime of financial security and success.

Creating an emergency fund and protecting your income streams are essential steps toward securing financial resilience. Together, they form a safety net that enables you to handle unexpected expenses, downturns, or interruptions in income without derailing your path to financial freedom. Building a reliable emergency fund gives you the flexibility to tackle sudden expenses without resorting to debt, while safeguarding your income streams provides the stability needed to consistently fund your savings and investments. Let's break down the importance of each aspect, with a look at the practical steps and mindset needed to keep you financially resilient.

Building a Reliable Emergency Fund: The Foundation of Financial Stability

Imagine you're driving across a vast stretch of desert. Halfway through your journey, your vehicle suddenly stalls, and you're miles from the nearest service station. Now, if you packed an extra fuel tank or a tool kit, you're likely equipped to handle the situation. But if you didn't, you're left stranded, hoping for help to come along. An emergency fund is that extra tank of fuel. It's what keeps you moving forward when unexpected financial "roadblocks" pop up, like medical bills, home repairs, or job loss.

Setting Your Emergency Fund Goal

An emergency fund is essentially a reserve of cash you set aside to cover unexpected expenses. Experts generally recommend that an emergency fund should cover three to six months' worth of living expenses. If you're self-employed or have variable income, it might be wise to aim for a slightly larger fund, up to nine or twelve months' worth of expenses.

To determine the amount you need, start by calculating your essential monthly expenses—things like rent or mortgage payments, utilities, food, insurance, and transportation. By knowing your baseline monthly expenses, you can set a clear, specific savings target for your emergency fund.

Creating Your Emergency Fund Step-by-Step

1. Start Small and Build Consistently: Building an emergency fund may seem daunting if you're just starting out, but consistency is key. Start with a manageable initial goal, like $500 or $1,000. Once you hit that milestone, work your way up to the three-to-six-month benchmark by contributing regularly.

2. Automate Your Savings: One of the simplest ways to build an emergency fund is by automating your savings. Set up automatic transfers from your checking account to a designated savings account each

month, ideally right after you receive your paycheck. This way, your emergency fund grows without you having to remember to make contributions.

3. Choose a Separate, Accessible Account: Keep your emergency fund in a high-yield savings account separate from your primary checking account. The high-yield savings account ensures your fund is accessible but not so easily tapped into for everyday expenses. This structure also provides some interest, allowing your fund to grow over time.

4. Reevaluate and Adjust Regularly: Your financial needs will evolve, so it's important to revisit and adjust your emergency fund periodically. For example, if you experience a change in expenses, such as taking on a mortgage, increasing your emergency fund might be a wise move to ensure you're fully protected.

## The Psychological Benefits of an Emergency Fund

Beyond its financial function, an emergency fund provides peace of mind. Knowing you have a safety net empowers you to make confident financial decisions without the constant worry of "what if" scenarios. This sense of security can also reduce stress during times of uncertainty, such as economic downturns or job changes. For instance, if an unexpected layoff occurs, your emergency fund allows you the time to search for a new opportunity without panicking about bills piling up.

## Protecting Your Income Streams: Diversification for Security

While an emergency fund is critical for handling unexpected costs, it's equally important to protect the very thing that funds it—your income streams. Relying on a single source of income, such as a full-time job, can leave you vulnerable if that job is disrupted. In contrast, having multiple income streams ensures that if one is affected, others can still provide financial support.

### Developing Multiple Income Streams

When it comes to income streams, diversity is key. Here are some common types:

- Primary Income: Your main source of income, typically from full-time employment or self-employment. This stream generally covers your core expenses.
- Secondary Income: This could include freelance work, consulting, or a side business. The income may be less predictable than a primary source, but it adds a valuable layer of financial security.

- Passive Income: Income that doesn't require active work to maintain, such as rental income, dividends, or interest. Building passive income streams takes time and upfront investment, but they are valuable in creating long-term financial resilience.

For example, let's consider David, a freelance graphic designer who started off solely relying on client work. Recognizing the potential risks, he diversified his income by creating and selling design templates on a digital marketplace. Even when client work slowed, David's passive income from template sales kept his finances stable, providing a cushion during lean months.

Safeguarding Your Income Streams

To protect and grow your income streams, consider the following strategies:

1. Invest in Skills that Boost Your Value: Constantly upgrade your skills to remain relevant and competitive in your field. For instance, if you're in tech, learning new programming languages or platforms can make you more marketable. The more adaptable and skilled you are, the less vulnerable you are to economic changes.

2. Build a Network to Open Opportunities: Networking opens doors to new income sources.

Building relationships in your industry and beyond can lead to opportunities like side gigs, partnerships, or even new job offers. A robust network enhances both your professional stability and income potential.

3. Create a Buffer for Your Income Streams: Just as you save for personal emergencies, consider creating a "business buffer" if you're self-employed or have a business. Having a few months' worth of business expenses set aside can help you navigate slow periods without relying on credit or dipping into your personal savings.

4. Stay Aware of Market Trends and Adapt: The job market and economic landscape change constantly. Staying informed about these shifts can help you identify emerging opportunities or potential risks. For instance, if your industry faces decline, consider pivoting to areas with greater growth prospects, such as transitioning from traditional marketing to digital marketing.

5. Consider Insurance as Income Protection: If you're self-employed, it's also wise to consider insurance options like income protection or business insurance. These can protect you from losing income if you're unable to work due to injury or illness. This added layer of security means that even if something happens to you, your finances remain secure.

Building Resilience with Financial Stability

Creating an emergency fund and protecting your income streams together form a powerful foundation of financial stability. Think of them as pillars holding up your financial house, making it strong and resilient to external forces. When you have a solid emergency fund and a diversified set of income streams, you're equipped to face financial storms and emerge stronger on the other side. These strategies provide more than just financial security—they enable you to pursue your goals with confidence, knowing that you're prepared for both the opportunities and challenges that may come your way.

By implementing these steps, you'll not only progress toward your first million but also establish lasting peace of mind on your financial journey. Financial freedom isn't just about wealth; it's about creating stability, resilience, and the ability to face whatever comes next with confidence.

Diversifying assets to reduce financial risks is a powerful strategy to protect and grow your wealth. Think of it as spreading your resources across different baskets so that if one of them falls, your entire financial future doesn't go down with it. Diversification, in essence, is about balance and adaptability—building a portfolio that can withstand the ups and downs of various markets. In this section, we'll explore how diversification works, its benefits, and real-life examples of individuals who've used it to secure and amplify their wealth.

## The Concept of Diversification: Why It Matters

Imagine you're a farmer planting a variety of crops—wheat, corn, and apples. Some years, the wheat might thrive, while corn production is low due to changes in weather or market demand. But because you're growing multiple crops, you're not solely dependent on any single harvest. If one crop fails, others may still succeed, allowing you to maintain stability in your livelihood. Diversifying assets works in the same way: by spreading your investments across different asset classes, you reduce the risk of a single market's downturn causing major financial damage.

Diversification isn't just about having different types of investments; it's about strategically choosing assets with varying levels of risk, performance, and liquidity so they balance each other. For instance, stocks are more volatile than bonds, and real estate typically has a lower liquidity level than mutual funds. By combining these in your portfolio, you create a mix that can perform steadily in changing economic conditions.

## The Benefits of Diversification

The primary benefit of diversification is that it mitigates risk. A diversified portfolio isn't immune to market declines, but it's better protected than a concentrated one. Here are a few benefits of diversification:

1. **Risk Reduction:** If you've invested solely in tech stocks and the tech market crashes, your entire portfolio suffers. But if your assets include real estate, bonds, and mutual funds, these other investments can buffer the loss. Diversification spreads out the impact of any single market's decline.

2. **Smoother Returns Over Time:** While individual asset classes can experience high volatility, a diversified portfolio typically enjoys smoother returns over time. This stability is particularly valuable for those investing for long-term goals, such as retirement.

3. **Increased Opportunity for Growth:** Diversification also gives you exposure to various growth opportunities. By investing in different sectors, you have a better chance of capturing gains from whichever sector is performing well. For example, if tech stocks are down, real estate or commodities might be on the rise, allowing your portfolio to benefit from different market conditions.

4. Peace of Mind: The psychological benefit of knowing your wealth isn't tied to a single investment is invaluable. Diversification offers reassurance that, even in tough economic times, your financial well-being is more secure.

Practical Steps to Diversify Your Assets

Building a diversified portfolio requires a blend of asset types, each serving a unique purpose. Here's how to approach diversification across some major categories:

1. Stocks (Equities): Stocks represent ownership in companies, providing potential for significant growth. They're typically considered higher-risk assets, as they're subject to market fluctuations, but they offer high returns over time. Within stocks, you can diversify further by investing in companies across sectors like technology, healthcare, finance, and consumer goods.

2. Bonds: Bonds are loans you make to corporations or governments, which pay you interest over a fixed period. They're usually lower-risk investments compared to stocks and provide regular income. Including bonds in your portfolio can help offset the volatility of stocks.

3. Real Estate: Real estate is a tangible asset that can provide rental income and potential appreciation. Real estate investments are valuable in a diversified portfolio because they often move independently of the stock market. You can invest in real estate directly by purchasing properties or indirectly through Real Estate Investment Trusts (REITs), which allow you to invest in real estate without the hassle of managing properties.

4. Commodities: Commodities include physical assets like gold, oil, and agricultural products. These assets can act as a hedge against inflation and provide additional diversification since their value isn't directly tied to stocks and bonds. Many investors use commodities like gold as a store of value during economic downturns.

5. Mutual Funds and ETFs: Mutual funds and ETFs (exchange-traded funds) pool money from multiple investors to invest in a diversified portfolio of assets. They're a popular choice for diversification because they allow you to invest in a broad range of assets with minimal effort. For example, an S&P 500 ETF invests in 500 large U.S. companies, giving you broad exposure to the stock market without having to pick individual stocks.

6. Alternative Investments: Depending on your risk tolerance, you might also consider alternative

investments like private equity, venture capital, or cryptocurrencies. These can offer substantial returns but are higher-risk and often less liquid, making them suitable for experienced investors with a high tolerance for risk.

Real-Life Example: Sarah's Diversified Portfolio

Sarah, a marketing professional in her late 30s, wanted to build wealth for the future while managing risk. She decided to build a diversified portfolio with different asset classes that balanced growth potential and stability. Here's how Sarah allocated her assets:

1. 40% in Stocks: Sarah invested in a mix of U.S. and international stocks, focusing on a variety of sectors. She bought shares in large tech companies, healthcare stocks, and a few emerging markets funds to capture growth in different parts of the world.

2. 25% in Bonds: Understanding the need for stability, Sarah allocated a quarter of her portfolio to bonds. She chose a mix of government and corporate bonds, providing regular interest payments and reducing her portfolio's overall volatility.

3. 20% in Real Estate: Sarah didn't want the responsibility of managing physical properties, so she invested in REITs. This decision allowed her to gain

exposure to real estate without the associated maintenance costs and responsibilities.

4. 10% in Commodities: Sarah included gold and other commodities as a hedge against inflation. She liked the idea that if the value of cash decreased, her commodities would likely retain their value.

5. 5% in Cryptocurrencies: Although a higher-risk asset, Sarah believed in the potential of cryptocurrencies. She invested a small percentage of her portfolio in Bitcoin and Ethereum to capture potential future gains while keeping her overall risk manageable.

Through this diversification, Sarah created a portfolio designed to withstand various market conditions. When the stock market fluctuated, her bonds and real estate holdings provided balance, and her commodities served as a hedge during inflationary periods.

Staying Disciplined with Diversification: Avoiding Over-Concentration

One challenge many investors face is over-concentration, which occurs when too much of a portfolio is allocated to one sector or asset class. Over time, an asset that performs well may grow to represent a large portion of the portfolio, increasing exposure to that specific market's risk. For instance, if tech stocks have performed exceptionally well, an investor might find that tech now dominates their portfolio. In these cases, "rebalancing" is essential.

Rebalancing is the process of adjusting your portfolio periodically to maintain your original asset allocation. For example, if stocks have grown and now make up 60% of your portfolio instead of the intended 50%, you might sell a portion of your stocks and reinvest in other asset classes, like bonds or real estate. This discipline helps you stick to your risk tolerance and long-term goals, rather than allowing short-term market performance to dictate your strategy.

Final Thoughts on Diversification

Diversifying assets isn't about chasing the next big investment trend; it's about building a stable, resilient portfolio. By carefully selecting a range of assets, you create financial protection, enabling you to weather economic downturns and even thrive when markets fluctuate. Diversification is a proactive approach to risk management that empowers you to maintain your path to financial freedom, knowing that you're prepared for both growth and challenge.

Through diversification, you not only reduce risk but also open the door to new growth opportunities. Every investment type brings unique characteristics to your portfolio, contributing to a balanced and strategic approach to wealth-building. Whether you're just starting to invest or re-evaluating your current portfolio, diversification is a powerful tool in creating sustainable financial success on your journey to that first million.

# CHAPTER 10

## The Final Stretch: Staying Motivated and Focused

As you approach the final stretch toward your first million, the journey transforms. Early on, your efforts were full of discovery—learning the importance of budgeting, setting goals, and diversifying your income. But now, with the finish line in sight, staying motivated and focused becomes crucial. For many, this stage can be a mix of excitement, exhaustion, and doubt. In this chapter, we'll explore how to maintain the drive to reach that milestone, avoid the pitfalls of complacency, and stay focused on the larger vision beyond the million-dollar mark.

### Understanding the Challenge of the Final Stretch

Imagine a marathon runner approaching the last few miles. The finish line is almost visible, and the energy of the crowd is invigorating. But it's also the hardest part of the race—the runner's legs are tired, their lungs are burning, and doubts begin to creep in. For those nearing their first million, the experience can be surprisingly similar. There's a mental and emotional aspect to this journey that is often underestimated.

At this stage, it's easy to feel like the hard part is over, leading some to slow down or lose focus. Financial temptations might grow stronger. As wealth accumulates, you may feel tempted to indulge in things you previously held off on. It's also natural to feel pressure to meet this goal sooner, leading to risky or impulsive decisions. This chapter provides strategies to maintain discipline, recalibrate your goals, and finish this journey with the focus and determination that brought you this far.

Setting Your Sights on the Bigger Vision

The first step in staying motivated is to remember the "why" behind your goal. Financial freedom is about more than a number in the bank. Revisit what this wealth means for your life—whether it's the freedom to work on your own terms, the ability to provide security for loved ones, or the potential to create a lasting impact on others.

Take Emily, a young entrepreneur who was on track to hit her first million. She found that the closer she came to her goal, the harder it was to stay focused. The excitement of hitting a financial milestone made her consider splurging on new luxuries or taking unnecessary business risks. What kept Emily on track was a vision board she created early in her journey. On this board, she placed images that represented what financial freedom meant to her: a family home, the logo of a charity she dreamed of supporting, and a picture of the beach where she hoped to take her parents on vacation. Each time she felt tempted to deviate, she looked at her board to reconnect with her original purpose.

Creating a vision board or a list of reasons for your goal can be a powerful motivator. Your purpose has likely evolved since you started, but staying connected to these goals can give you the focus you need to push through the final stretch.

## The Power of Micro-Goals for Staying Motivated

While the finish line is close, a million dollars is still a big number. Breaking down this larger goal into smaller, actionable micro-goals can make the journey feel more achievable. Each step toward these smaller targets generates a sense of accomplishment, keeping you motivated.

For instance, say you're $100,000 away from reaching your first million. Rather than focusing solely on this larger number, try setting weekly or monthly savings and investment goals. This might mean aiming to increase your portfolio by a certain percentage, finding new investment opportunities, or seeking an additional income source for that month. When you reach each smaller milestone, celebrate the win. These small victories build momentum and keep you engaged.

Consider the story of Raj, a software developer and investor. With $950,000 in net worth, Raj knew he was close to his million-dollar goal but felt overwhelmed by the pressure to reach that last stretch. He decided to set incremental savings targets—every $10,000 he saved or earned was marked as a victory. By treating these steps as small wins, Raj found joy in the process rather than feeling bogged down by the larger goal.

Avoiding the Trap of Complacency

As you approach financial milestones, complacency can creep in. A sense of accomplishment can sometimes lead to relaxing your standards or assuming that future success is guaranteed. This mindset can be dangerous, as it often leads to unnecessary risks, unchecked spending, or missed opportunities.

To avoid this, commit to maintaining the habits and discipline that brought you this far. Track your spending, manage your budget, and regularly assess your investments. It's easy to feel tempted to "live a little" when your bank account reflects the results of your hard work. But remember that financial freedom isn't just about reaching one milestone; it's about securing long-term stability.

Take the example of Jake, a business owner who started celebrating his growing wealth by investing in luxury items and neglecting his budget. His expenses slowly crept up, and he soon found himself dipping into savings to cover lifestyle costs. Recognizing the danger, Jake revisited his original goals and reset his financial practices, reaffirming his commitment to managing his wealth responsibly.

The Role of Routine in Maintaining Focus

Staying focused on long-term financial goals requires structure. Establishing daily, weekly, or monthly routines can help you remain disciplined, ensuring you regularly evaluate your finances and adjust as needed.

Here are some routines to consider:

1. Daily Financial Review: Spend a few minutes each day reviewing transactions and ensuring spending aligns with your budget.
2. Weekly Investment Check-In: Dedicate time to review your portfolio, researching market trends or rebalancing if needed.

3. Monthly Goal Tracking: At the end of each month, assess your progress toward your million-dollar goal. Note any wins, losses, and lessons learned, and adjust your strategies accordingly.

Routines are powerful because they create momentum and foster habits that keep you accountable. For instance, if reviewing your investments becomes a weekly ritual, you're less likely to make impulsive decisions when market changes arise.

Finding Strength in Community

Financial journeys can sometimes feel isolating, particularly as you move closer to your goal. Engaging with a community of like-minded individuals can provide support, accountability, and inspiration. Seek out groups or forums where people share similar financial goals, such as investment clubs, wealth-building communities, or mentorship groups.

Take Mia, who was only $50,000 away from her first million but felt unsure about how to navigate the final stretch. She joined an online community of investors and entrepreneurs, where people shared stories about staying motivated. Through conversations and advice, she found inspiration to stay focused, even during moments of doubt. This support system gave Mia the extra motivation to stick with her plans and avoid unnecessary risks.

## Embracing the Journey, Not Just the Destination

When your goal is within reach, it's easy to focus solely on the destination. But true fulfillment comes from appreciating the journey itself. Achieving your first million is a significant milestone, but it's also a stepping stone toward even bigger dreams. Reflect on the skills you've gained, the discipline you've built, and the growth you've experienced.

Consider journaling about your progress and celebrating small wins. Reflecting on your journey can help you see how far you've come, reinforcing the sense of accomplishment and pride in your achievements. This mindset shift can transform the process from something to "get through" into something to celebrate and enjoy.

### Visualizing Beyond the Million

One of the most motivating strategies in the final stretch is to start envisioning life beyond the million. Think about how you'll manage and grow this wealth, what causes or passions you'd like to invest in, or new business ventures you hope to start. The first million is a launching pad; it's what comes after that will define the legacy of your financial journey.

The final stretch toward your first million is both a celebration and a challenge. Staying motivated and focused requires intention, discipline, and a strong connection to your purpose. As you near your goal, remember that this journey is about more than just the number—it's about the freedom, security, and opportunities that await.

Stay committed, stay humble, and, above all, stay excited about what lies ahead. Your first million is not the end but the beginning of a life filled with possibility, impact, and growth. The finish line is in sight—now it's time to cross it with confidence, knowing that your best financial days are just beginning.

Learning from setbacks and maintaining motivation is one of the most challenging yet rewarding skills on the path to financial freedom. In the journey toward your first million, setbacks aren't just possibilities—they're almost inevitable. They come in many forms: an unexpected dip in the market, a failed business venture, or an investment that doesn't pan out. While setbacks can feel discouraging, they also present some of the greatest opportunities for growth, resilience, and learning.

Embracing Setbacks as Stepping Stones

Imagine Alex, a young entrepreneur who started a small e-commerce business selling eco-friendly products. Alex had high hopes, investing his savings into launching the business. The first few months were promising; he secured a decent number of customers, and reviews were positive. But then, a major supplier ran into logistical issues, leading to delays, product shortages, and customer complaints. Alex tried to manage the crisis, but sales dropped significantly, and the momentum he had worked so hard to build seemed to crumble.

Initially, Alex felt defeated, questioning whether he was truly cut out for entrepreneurship. But as he reflected on the experience, he realized there were valuable lessons embedded in the setback. He learned the importance of building a diversified supplier network, creating a contingency fund, and managing customer expectations. Instead of viewing the setback as a failure, he reframed it as a lesson that would serve him in the long run.

Learning from setbacks means changing your perspective on what failure truly is. Rather than a dead-end, setbacks become checkpoints—moments of recalibration and growth. They provide valuable insights into what works and what doesn't and offer lessons that, if embraced, prevent similar mistakes in the future. By looking at setbacks this way, you turn challenges into stepping stones, each one bringing you closer to your goal.

Building Resilience Through Adversity

Resilience is the capacity to keep going, even when faced with repeated challenges. For Sarah, a corporate executive working toward financial independence, resilience became her guiding principle. Sarah diligently saved, invested in mutual funds, and worked extra hours to build her portfolio. Then, a family medical emergency forced her to dip into her savings, setting her back years in her plan.

Initially, the setback left her feeling frustrated and defeated. It felt as though she had taken several steps backward after years of hard work. But as she processed her emotions, she realized the setback had given her a new sense of purpose. She knew she had to keep going, not just for her own financial goals but also to be in a better position to support her family in the future.

Instead of letting adversity keep her down, Sarah rebuilt her strategy with even more determination. She adjusted her budget, increased her investment contributions, and diversified her portfolio to add a safety net. Her resilience transformed what could have been a complete derailment into a lesson on flexibility and adaptability. This resilience gave Sarah not just financial stability but also the peace of mind that she could handle whatever life threw her way.

Learning to Adapt and Pivot

Sometimes, setbacks signal the need to adjust your strategy. That's what happened to Mark, who started as a freelance graphic designer and dreamed of building a creative agency. His goal was to expand quickly, bringing in a team to help with his increasing workload. But when he took on more clients than he could handle, the quality of work suffered, and he started losing clients instead of gaining them. The setback was unexpected and painful, especially after the time and money he had invested in his agency.

Instead of quitting, Mark decided to pivot. He reduced his client load, focused on improving his services, and reinvested in building a portfolio that showcased his best work. He learned that growth didn't have to be rapid to be successful. By learning from this setback, Mark developed a more sustainable approach to his business, focusing on quality over quantity. In time, he began attracting clients who valued his work, and his business grew at a steady pace.

Setbacks often reveal flaws in our strategies or assumptions, teaching us the importance of adaptability. When we approach setbacks with a mindset of curiosity rather than judgment, we create the space to explore alternative paths and pivot as needed. This flexibility is an invaluable asset, particularly in the pursuit of long-term financial goals, where unexpected market changes and life events require us to adjust our course.

Keeping the Bigger Picture in Focus

One of the most difficult aspects of facing setbacks is the loss of motivation that often follows. After a setback, it can feel like all the work you've done has gone to waste. But maintaining motivation comes down to remembering why you started the journey in the first place and seeing each setback as just one part of a much larger story.

Consider Jenna, a teacher who was investing in stocks as a way to build wealth outside of her teaching salary. After a promising start, she experienced a market downturn that severely impacted her portfolio. Frustrated, Jenna considered selling off her remaining shares to cut her losses. But after speaking with her mentor, she was reminded of her long-term goal: financial freedom and the ability to retire early.

This setback was a difficult moment, but her mentor helped her see it as a part of the natural cycle of investing. Rather than focusing on the loss, Jenna realigned her perspective to view the market downturn as an opportunity to buy shares at lower prices. She kept her bigger picture in mind, using this setback to strengthen her commitment to long-term growth rather than immediate results. This perspective helped her not only recover financially but also deepen her understanding of investing, which became a valuable skill she carried forward.

When we look beyond the immediate impact of setbacks, they become less daunting. Remembering the "why" behind our goals gives us a sense of purpose that goes beyond temporary obstacles.

Celebrating Progress, No Matter How Small

Setbacks can make progress feel like an uphill battle. When we're faced with delays or challenges, it's easy to overlook how far we've come. One way to counteract the discouragement that setbacks bring is to celebrate small victories along the way.

Alexis, a single mother working toward her financial freedom goal, knew she'd have to handle both financial and personal challenges. During a period when her business faced cash flow issues, she felt discouraged and was close to giving up. But her coach encouraged her to celebrate even the small wins —like paying off a small debt or setting aside a modest amount in savings.

Recognizing these victories helped Alexis keep her momentum going, even when her progress felt slow. She realized that every small step mattered, and each one brought her closer to her ultimate goal. This shift in perspective made her setbacks feel less discouraging and her successes more meaningful.

Celebrating progress is a way of acknowledging the journey itself. Setbacks may slow down the pace, but they don't erase the steps you've already taken. Recognizing and celebrating these small achievements creates motivation and keeps you moving forward.

Turning Setbacks into Strengths

As you navigate the final stretch of your financial journey, setbacks become more than just hurdles; they become experiences that build resilience, adaptability, and wisdom. Learning from setbacks and maintaining motivation through these challenges shapes who you become along the way. By embracing these obstacles and viewing them as learning opportunities, you're not only getting closer to your financial goals but also developing the mental strength and discipline that will sustain your wealth over the long term.

The true value of setbacks lies in their ability to reveal new perspectives, test your commitment, and strengthen your determination. In the pursuit of your first million, setbacks are not detours—they're essential stops along the way that bring you closer to the best version of yourself. By learning to navigate these challenges, you're building the kind of resilience that will carry you beyond the million and into a lifetime of financial growth and success.

Transitioning from achieving your first million to reaching even greater financial goals is an exciting phase, but it requires a new mindset, refined strategies, and a commitment to continuous growth. For many, the journey from zero to one million is the hardest part; it's filled with lessons on saving, investing, risk-taking, and resilience. Once that first milestone is achieved, the next steps are about scaling, sustainability, and smart financial management. Here's how successful individuals have made that leap, and practical tips to follow on your own journey from your first million to even greater financial goals.

Revisiting Your Goals and Setting New Milestones

Consider Emma, an engineer who saved and invested wisely to reach her first million by her early 40s. Achieving this goal was exhilarating, but she quickly realized she needed a new direction. Reaching her first million wasn't an end in itself; it was just a foundation. After taking some time to celebrate, Emma sat down to reevaluate her financial goals. She asked herself what she wanted in the next ten years: Was it a comfortable early retirement? Or did she want to build generational wealth for her children?

Emma's journey illustrates the importance of revisiting your goals once you hit that first milestone. Set new milestones—whether that means working toward five million, ten million, or creating a passive income that covers your living expenses entirely. Expanding your financial horizons involves thinking beyond immediate wealth and envisioning a broader, more impactful goal.

To successfully transition from your first million to higher levels of wealth, regularly reassess and update your goals. This ensures you're not just accumulating wealth aimlessly but moving forward with a purpose, aligning with what truly matters to you.

Scaling Your Income Streams

One of the keys to moving beyond your first million is building upon the income streams that got you there. Michael, a corporate executive, reached his first million through a mix of his salary, stock investments, and a side business consulting startups. But rather than staying comfortable, Michael looked for ways to expand. He decided to scale his consulting business by hiring a small team, allowing him to take on more clients without having to handle everything himself. He also leveraged his executive experience to secure higher-paying speaking engagements and started building a personal brand online.

Michael's approach demonstrates that scaling isn't about reinventing the wheel; it's about amplifying what already works. Look at the income streams that contributed to your first million and ask how you can take them further. If you're a business owner, consider expanding into new markets or developing additional products or services. If you're an investor, consider diversifying into assets like real estate or venture capital to enhance your portfolio.

Scaling often requires reinvestment, whether that's putting money into marketing, hiring skilled people, or expanding into new verticals. By focusing on what you're already good at, you're setting yourself up for more sustainable growth rather than starting from scratch.

Leveraging Compound Growth for Accelerated Gains

One of the greatest benefits of reaching your first million is the ability to leverage compound growth on a larger scale. Compounding works exponentially, meaning the more capital you have, the faster it can grow. Sarah, an early retiree who built her wealth through disciplined stock market investments, understood this well. She let her investments sit, adding a portion of her annual returns back into her portfolio, which allowed her capital to snowball over time. Her million turned into two million, then three, all without additional input beyond her initial investments and modest reinvestment.

The power of compound growth accelerates once you reach a larger principal amount, so make it work for you by reinvesting gains, avoiding premature withdrawals, and giving your assets time to mature. If you're in stocks, aim to hold long-term positions in high-quality companies or ETFs that historically show strong growth. In real estate, allow properties to appreciate while reinvesting rental income back into the market. Whatever your preferred investment, let your first million compound, and stay consistent to build momentum.

Expanding Your Financial Literacy

Reaching your first million undoubtedly required some degree of financial literacy, but moving to greater wealth means expanding that knowledge base. When James, a self-made entrepreneur, reached his first million, he realized he couldn't rely solely on his instincts anymore; he needed expert guidance to avoid costly mistakes. He began attending seminars, took online courses, and even pursued a certification in financial planning to manage his growing wealth more effectively.

To successfully transition beyond your first million, broaden your knowledge in areas like tax planning, asset protection, and advanced investment strategies. Consider consulting with financial advisors, tax planners, and attorneys who specialize in wealth management. As your portfolio becomes more complex, you'll benefit from professional insights, allowing you to make well-informed decisions that protect and grow your wealth.

Developing a Balanced Approach to Risk

Moving beyond your first million often involves a more strategic approach to risk. Jennifer, a tech executive who had saved her first million, was initially hesitant to take big risks. But she realized that staying entirely conservative wouldn't yield the same growth potential as her earlier years. Instead, Jennifer allocated a portion of her portfolio to higher-risk, higher-reward investments like startups and tech stocks, while keeping the majority in safer assets.

A balanced approach means evaluating how much risk you're comfortable with as you build wealth.

Diversify your portfolio by including a mix of assets with varying risk levels, like bonds, blue-chip stocks, high-growth companies, and real estate. Adjust your risk tolerance based on your age, financial goals, and current life situation. By thoughtfully balancing risks, you position yourself to capture growth while protecting your core assets.

Practicing Patience and Long-Term Thinking

Once you've reached your first million, the journey to higher wealth requires patience and a long-term outlook. Nick, an investor with a goal of ten million, learned this the hard way. Early on, he frequently checked his portfolio and made impulsive decisions based on market fluctuations, which actually stunted his progress. It wasn't until he adopted a longer-term perspective—allowing his investments to ride out market cycles—that he saw significant gains.

To achieve wealth beyond the first million, practice patience. Avoid reacting to daily market news or short-term economic changes. Establish a long-term strategy and stay disciplined. Wealth accumulation at this stage is more of a marathon than a sprint, and by keeping your focus on the bigger picture, you avoid emotional decisions that can derail your progress.

Protecting Your Wealth and Preparing for Legacy Building

As your wealth grows, so does the need for protection. Many people who reach higher levels of wealth, like Taylor, a physician turned investor, prioritize safeguarding their assets to ensure their hard-earned success isn't compromised. Taylor set up trusts for his children, invested in asset protection insurance, and worked with an estate planner to ensure his wealth would benefit future generations.

Protecting your wealth goes beyond just smart investing—it includes legal strategies to shield assets from lawsuits, excessive taxation, or unforeseen liabilities. Once you've reached a certain level of financial security, legacy planning becomes essential. Think about how you want your wealth to impact future generations, charitable causes, or communities you care about. Setting up trusts, planning estates, and creating charitable foundations are all options that help preserve and direct your wealth according to your values.

Maintaining Humility and a Growth-Oriented Mindset

One of the most valuable qualities you can maintain as you grow your wealth is humility. After reaching his first million, Marcus, an entrepreneur, fell into the trap of complacency. Believing he had "made it," he became less attentive to his financial discipline, and his wealth stagnated. Eventually, Marcus recognized his need to keep learning and growing. He refocused, sought new skills, and surrounded himself with mentors who held him accountable.

No matter how much wealth you accumulate, staying humble and curious is key. Avoid letting success breed complacency; instead, use it as motivation to keep pushing your boundaries. The financial landscape is constantly evolving, and a growth-oriented mindset will help you stay ahead, continuously finding new ways to optimize and build upon what you've already achieved.

The journey from your first million to even greater wealth is one of refinement, strategy, and purpose. By setting new goals, scaling income streams, leveraging compound growth, expanding financial literacy, balancing risk, practicing patience, protecting assets, and maintaining a growth mindset, you're not just preserving your wealth but actively building on it. This transition is about making smart, thoughtful decisions that not only sustain but accelerate your financial freedom—turning your first million into a powerful foundation for even greater financial achievements.

# ABOUT THE AUTHOR

**Mukesh Alex Vaidya is an Amazon bestselling author of fiction and nonfiction**

He is a techie-turned author of fiction and nonfiction books. The Secret of Hiram based on the legend of Hiram who built the Temple of Solomon hit the Amazon bestseller list. His nonfiction Bootstrap Dream How to start a tech company from scratch is an authoritative work on startups.

His goal in life is to inspire the readers to follow their dreams and help them to step out of the rat race and live life to the fullest. He follows a simple and lucid writing style and lyrical language.

Born in Kollam, Kerala, he was a voracious reader. He is very passionate about writing and telling stories. He is a curious Author who explores different themes and motifs. As part of the writing process, he loves immersing himself in the books diving headfirst into research and writing organically. He loves history, legends, and myths.